T0231389

Impact of Technology on Resource Sharing: Experimentation and Maturity

Impact of Technology on Resource Sharing: Experimentation and Maturity

Thomas C. Wilson
Editor

 CRC Press
Taylor & Francis Group
Boca Raton London New York

CRC Press is an imprint of the
Taylor & Francis Group, an informa business

Impact of Technology on Resource Sharing: Experimentation and Maturity has also been published as *Resource Sharing & Information Networks*, Volume 8, Number 1 1992.

© 1992 by The Haworth Press, Inc. All rights reserved. No part of this work may be reproduced or utilized in any form or by any means, electronic or mechanical, including photocopying, microfilm and recording, or by any information storage and retrieval system, without permission in writing from the publisher. Printed in the United States of America.

Reprinted 2009 by CRC Press

Library of Congress Cataloging-in-Publication Data

Impact of technology on resource sharing : experimentation and maturity / Thomas C. Wilson, editor.
  p. cm.
  "Has also been published as Resource sharing & information networks, volume 8, number 1, 1992"-T.p. verso.
  Includes bibliographical references.
  ISBN 1-56024-391-0 (H : acid free paper)
  1. Library cooperation–United States. 2. Libraries–United States–Data processing. 3. Library information networks–United States. I. Wilson, Thomas C. (Thomas Carl), 1958- .
Z731.I48 1992
021.6'4–dc20
                            92-33112
                              CIP

Impact of Technology on Resource Sharing: Experimentation and Maturity

CONTENTS

An Annotated Bibliography on Networking: Past, Present, and Future   **159**
Patricia A. Kreitz

ABOUT THE EDITOR

Thomas C. Wilson, MILS, is Head of Systems for the University of Houston Libraries, where he is responsible for planning and supporting all data communications and computing in the libraries. Nationally known for speaking and writing on networking and CD-ROM, he began his work at the University of Houston in the Information Services Department as a Social Sciences Reference Librarian/Bibliographer and was later appointed Coordinator of the Computerized Information Retrieval Services Program. Previously, Mr. Wilson served as Technology and Marketing Specialist for a major database producer, Assistant Librarian in a medical library, and Project Associate for a grant-funded, state-wide computer literacy program.

Experimentation and Maturity:
A Prelude to Cycles

Thomas C. Wilson

A good starting point for any intellectual endeavor is the definition of terms. Unfortunately, resource sharing has acquired an unnecessarily limited scope. Indeed, if one conducts a cursory literature search using the phrase "resource sharing," one is likely to retrieve items that deal mostly with interlibrary loan. While ILL represents one type of resource sharing, it does not exhaust the totality of the concept. In fact, some would argue that ILL, as presently conceived and implemented, cannot hope to survive in this electronic information age. Perhaps then a broader definition of resource sharing is in order.

The other phrase for this intellectual endeavor that requires definition, or perhaps a context, is "technological development." Any review of technological development will eventually touch political, philosophical, social, financial, legal, managerial, and attitudinal issues. And whether a particular development is experimental or widely implemented (i.e., mature), its value will necessarily be determined in the face of these issues and not on purely technical merits. Furthermore, the degree to which a discussion focuses on these broader issues is inversely proportional to the likelihood of consensus. Rather than to suggest that the impact of recent technological developments on resource sharing can be

Thomas C. Wilson is Head of Systems at the University of Houston Libraries, Houston, TX 77204-2091 and Editor of this volume.

The editor would like to thank Jeff Fadell for his grammatical and editorial consultation, Robert Holley for his encouragement and support, and Caryn Wilson for her time and patience.

© 1992 by The Haworth Press, Inc. All rights reserved.

1

examined without addressing these other important issues, the editor prefers to cast the reader into the middle of these junctures in order to provoke thought and discussion among the greater library community.

Libraries traditionally have represented a unique blend of preservation and adaptation. In other words, while these institutions have sought to maintain materials and procedures of the past, they have also frequently been the pioneering implementors of technological change. Nearly everyone who has worked in libraries, or used them regularly, can relate stories that exemplify either of the extremes on this preserve-adapt continuum. The very institutional soul of libraries is defined by this ongoing tension. One could even say that every decision made in a library is an illustration of this bi-polar, existential struggle and that libraries tend to cycle back and forth between the extremes.

At the current point in time, however, the outcome of this struggle, both for individual libraries and for the library community as a whole, is especially critical. Never before has so much rested on the near-term decisions made by libraries. Other interests, external to libraries, have become major players in the information industry, and users will go to them if the services offered are deemed relevant and timely. These entities, in some cases, present significant threats to libraries as traditionally conceived.

Changes in the world around libraries present challenges. Internal change is also evident. Wetherbee details a gradual shift underway that places greater emphasis on the local shared system database than on a national system, as traditionally represented by the major bibliographic utilities. This trend would suggest the possibility of a deteriorating national source for cataloging and holdings information, a fundamental element of nearly all resource sharing arrangements to date. Some may view this outcome as positive since it also reflects the fact that more sophisticated local systems are installed. Others, Rush for example, argue that more centralization (i.e., less local variance) is needed for libraries to realize more fully the benefit of resource sharing. The goal of the latter seems at odds with the destiny of the former.

While CD-ROM could hardly be considered an experimental technology at this point in time, much experimentation with it continues. For example, Thompson and Horton describe the use of CD-ROM as a medium for union catalogs, while Joy and Schwartz examine the application of this technology to collection evaluation and development. These authors remind the reader that the technology is a tool. With any technology, stability begets feasibility, but applications breed maturity.

The extent to which small-scale systems (e.g., high-powered workstations and servers) have been implemented as platforms for library applications might suggest that large-scale systems no longer exist. Such is not the case. Wetherbee's survey of twenty-nine local systems demonstrates that many large-scale systems are still in use. Sloan also supports this notion in his discussion of ILLINET Online, an example of established, large-scale computing. Even in this "mature" environment, adaptations are taking place to further enhance resource sharing in terms of both traditional interlibrary lending and experimental system interconnection.

Networking technologies have also influenced resource sharing over the past two decades. In the library community, however, the definition of the term "network" has been at best confused, and at worst, conceptually misleading. Readers must mentally retain the difference between networks as human institutions brokering services, such as PALINET, and networks as technical infrastructure. These definitional variances are likely to become even fuzzier over the next few decades as networking technologies advance to a point where the separation of a user from an application from an address from a transport mechanism from a host/server will become irrelevant to most people.

Connectivity, networking as its most basic level, plays an important role in fostering resource sharing. At the heart of connectivity are standards. There are more standards in the library community than can be covered in a single volume. One of the most promising is Z39.50. Although it has been under development for over ten years, only recently have real implementations of the protocol been tested successfully. Needleman outlines the protocol and its potential for supporting and enhancing inter-system connectivity, another example of resource sharing.

The impact of large-scale networking can be appreciated only by viewing the applications it makes possible. National and international network infrastructure, as depicted by BITNET, USENET, and the Internet, support a broad range of resource sharing activities. Meizel presents several that address a fundamental need of society, namely, enhancing the educational process for high schoolers. Summerhill further outlines options for the library community.

Under the surface of these technical discussions, however, emerge non-technical (or less technical) issues, as previously mentioned. These issues necessarily color decisions made in libraries. One thing is clear: libraries struggle with existing budgets. The technologies described in this volume and elsewhere do not come cheaply. Thus, once again, libraries are faced with challenges to budgetary philosophies. The basic technical connectivity that supports resource sharing in an electronic environment is not available across the board. To create global connectivity is no small endeavor. Fortunately, the library community does not need to achieve this in a vacuum, although the history of library automation suggests that many have tried. Nonetheless, for some libraries significant investments will be required. One perspective of funding this progress is presented by Rush.

What does the future hold? Perhaps the library community can gain an enlightened perspective by viewing the ground it has traversed in the past. Kreitz offers an annotated bibliography with a twist: it is arranged chronologically within broad subject categories to provide the reader with a thread of historical development. There are multiple futures available and rich histories to support them. And so the cycle continues–experimentation and maturity.

A Union Catalog on CD-ROM: Tool for Resource Sharing? The Houston Area Research Library Consortium CD-ROM Union Catalog Project

Linda L. Thompson
Keiko Cho Horton

SUMMARY. This article outlines the development of the Houston Area Research Library Consortium's CD-ROM union catalog, presents hypotheses on the impact of the union catalog on resource sharing generally among the Consortium members and specifically with regard to the University of Houston Libraries, and examines these hypotheses in relation to the preliminary data. The examination reveals that currently available data do not support the hypotheses. The process of evaluating the data and other evidence of the catalog's effects, however, have caused the authors to reconsider the terms used to define the catalog's impact and to propose alternative avenues of investigation.

INTRODUCTION

In May 1990, the initial version of the Houston Area Research Library Consortium union catalog on CD-ROM was delivered to member libraries. The union catalog was designed to serve as a back-up for each library's online catalog and to facilitate resource

Linda L. Thompson is Assistant Director for Bibliographic Services and Keiko Cho Horton is Coordinator of Interlibrary Loan Services for the University of Houston Libraries, Houston, TX 77204-2091.

© 1992 by The Haworth Press, Inc. All rights reserved.

sharing among Consortium libraries through state-of-the-art technology. As such, it was anticipated that access to the union catalog would have a significant impact on interlibrary borrowing and lending among the participating libraries. This article outlines the development of the union catalog, presents hypotheses on the effect of the union catalog on resource sharing, and then examines these hypotheses in the light of the preliminary data available.

BACKGROUND

The Houston Area Research Library Consortium (HARLiC) was formed in 1978 for the purpose of meeting the research and information needs of the Houston community by sharing library collections and services. Eight libraries form the membership of the Consortium: Houston Academy of Medicine-Texas Medical Center Library, Houston Public Library, Prairie View A&M University Library, Rice University Fondren Library, Texas A&M University Evans Library, Texas Southern University Library, University of Houston Libraries, and University of Texas at Galveston Medical Branch Library. HARLiC is governed by a Board consisting of the directors of the member libraries; committees and task forces appointed by the Board are instrumental in developing and implementing projects to further the goals of the Consortium.

The HARLiC libraries have cooperated on several resource sharing endeavors during the Consortium's existence. Chief among these are a union list of serials on OCLC, a courier service that delivers and picks up library materials at each library on a regular basis (daily for the libraries in Houston and twice weekly for the remaining libraries), and a limited reciprocal borrowing agreement. The union catalog on CD-ROM represents the most recent effort to enhance resource sharing within the Consortium.

The idea for the HARLiC CD-ROM union catalog first began to take shape five or six years ago. Initially some member libraries were interested in creating back-ups for their online catalogs and thought that CD-ROM technology might offer the best solution. As staff from the various HARLiC libraries discussed this concept, it became apparent that a cooperative effort would have several advantages. Not only would each library achieve its initial goal of acquiring a back-up system for its online public access catalog, but a cooperative project would produce a union catalog of the more than eight million volumes jointly held by the Consortium libraries which would be accessible to the patrons of each member library. Additionally, the cost to each library would be less in a joint project than it would be if each library produced its own independent CD-ROM catalog. It was generally agreed that a union catalog would be an enhancement for library operations and services, although no concrete strategy was developed to exploit the potential usefulness of this tool. A union catalog seemed to complement the cooperative efforts that HARLiC had already undertaken. Even without a detailed agenda, the Consortium members had been working successfully toward greater sharing of one another's collections since the Consortium's formation.

DEVELOPMENT AND IMPLEMENTATION

In the fall of 1987 a task force was appointed, with one representative from each library, to develop specifications for a CD-ROM union catalog. These specifications would form the basis of the Request for Proposal (RFP). Simultaneously a grant proposal was prepared seeking funding from the Department of Education under the newly created College Library Technology and Cooperation Grants Program (HEA Title II-D), the first of which were to be awarded the next federal fiscal year. HARLiC was one of the initial recipients of these grants in the amount of $100,000 for a two-year period.

The RFP was issued in early 1988 with three responses received: Auto-graphics, BroDart, and Marcive. After demonstrations and product evaluations were conducted, a recommendation was made to the HARLiC Board of Directors resulting in the selection of Marcive in August 1988. Marcive was chosen because the task force thought the product's design contributed to a markedly faster response time, and the user interface was more readily comprehensible. Additionally, Marcive had considerable experience with medical libraries (including manipulation of NLM call numbers and Medical Subject Headings), and previous experience working with the non-standard machine-readable bibliographic records of one of the participating libraries.

Delays were encountered at each step of the process. Extended contract negotiations with the vendor postponed signing the contract. In addition, each library needed more time than expected to deliver its database to the vendor. The resolution of problems encountered with the search software and the test CD-ROM database required more time and effort than anticipated. Many of these problems arose from misunderstandings between HARLiC and the vendor regarding the correct method to use for locating, processing, and displaying holdings information contained in the bibliographic record. Other problems occurred because of the past cataloging practices employed by some libraries. Some records did not appear or interact with the search software as expected, a rude reminder of these practices. All of these problems were exacerbated by the need to coordinate information among the seven participating HARLiC libraries prior to communicating with Marcive.[1] At times, this situation added days to the communication process.

After overcoming these initial difficulties the contract was signed in May 1989. The initial catalog containing 1.75 million unique bibliographic records was delivered one year later. The first updated version of the catalog was completed in May 1991 and contained approximately 2.1 million records. In the future, it is anticipated that a new catalog will be produced semi-annually.

The only library of the HARLiC member libraries to implement the catalog immediately for both staff and public users on any significant scale was the University of Houston Libraries. Over the course of the summer of 1990, more than twenty workstations were installed. It was assumed that availability of the catalog to UH Libraries users and staff, particularly interlibrary loan and reference staff, would have some impact on interlibrary borrowing by UH from the other HARLiC libraries. Also, since the library holdings for Rice University had not yet been included, it was hypothesized that this lack of information would impact specifically on borrowing by UH from Rice.

DATA ANALYSIS

At this time, the data are preliminary. Although courier delivery statistics are available from which ILL activity can be inferred, there are no statistics for on-site transactions using the reciprocal borrowing arrangements among HARLiC libraries. A thorough study of catalog use has also not been done. Interestingly enough, the initial data accumulated through spring semester 1991 do not support any of the hypotheses: (1) that use of the HARLiC union catalog by University of Houston library users and staff would have a significant positive correlation with HARLiC interlibrary borrowing by UH in comparison with UH HARLiC borrowing for previous years, or in comparison with overall UH ILL borrowing statistics for the same period or for previous years; and (2) that the lack of library holdings for Rice University in the HARLiC union catalog would impact negatively on the amount of borrowing done by the University of Houston Libraries from Rice University when compared with previous levels of activity.[2]

The projected level of UH HARLiC ILL borrowing activity for academic year 1990/91 represents a decrease of 8.6% when compared with the previous year and of 11.2% from the 1988/89 academic year (Figure 1). Simultaneously, the projected level of overall ILL borrowing activity for UH Libraries indicates increases of 31.4% and 33.6% respectively over the two previous years (Figure 2). HARLiC borrowing as a percentage of overall ILL borrowing for 1990/91 has decreased significantly as well: from 34.6% of total ILL borrowing in 1988/89 to a projected 23% for 1990/91 (Figures 3a, 3b).

Borrowing of Rice University library materials by the UH community increased over this same period: by 53.3% over 1989/90 and by 29.2% compared with 1988/89 (Figures 4, 5). Borrowing from Rice now accounts for 28.4% of all HARLiC borrowing by UH Libraries compared with 19.5% two years ago (Figures 6a, 6b). Similarly, borrowing by Texas A&M University from Rice University for the same periods increased by 75.6% and 46.5% respectively. The same borrowing pattern is evident for most of the other HARLiC libraries (Figure 7). Clearly the absence of Rice University's bibliographic records in the HARLiC union catalog

FIGURE 1

UH HARLiC ILL Borrowing

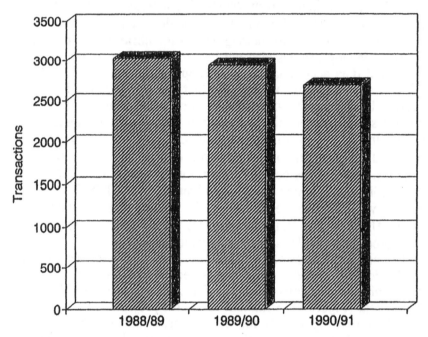

did not have a negative impact on borrowing from this collection by the other members of the Consortium.

Additionally, the total number of HARLiC ILL transactions by all HARLiC libraries has remained fairly constant for the past several years (Figure 8). The University of Houston Libraries, the only member of HARLiC that has experienced a widespread implementation of the union catalog thus far, however, has experienced a reduction in HARLiC ILL transactions while its overall level of ILL activity has increased (Figure 9).

The above findings, as well as the additional information contained in the HARLiC ILL statistics, raise questions about the shifting borrowing-to-lending ratios within HARLiC and what these changes mean. Some of the interesting trends discovered while

FIGURE 2

UH ILL Borrowing

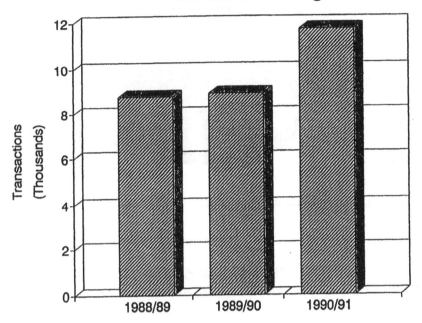

examining the data include the fact that both Texas Southern University Library and Rice University Fondren Library are net lenders and Texas A&M University Evans Library is a net borrower, while the other member libraries are operating more nearly on a one-for-one basis. Do the libraries of Texas Southern and Rice universities meet the needs of their users more effectively than the other HARLiC libraries, while the library of Texas A&M is not sufficient for its users' needs? Or is interlibrary loan service promoted more heavily at Texas A&M (and thereby used to good advantage) than is the case at the other libraries? These issues, and other similar ones, need to be investigated in a future study.

No ready explanations present themselves regarding the decrease in UH borrowing from other HARLiC libraries as a whole while accompanied by an increase in borrowing from Rice. In an attempt

FIGURE 3a

UH ILL Borrowing
1988/89

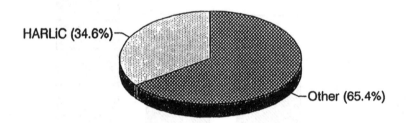

Total transactions = 8,762

FIGURE 3b

UH ILL Borrowing
1990/91 (projected)

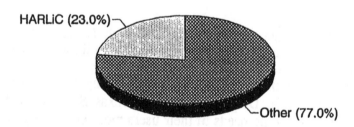

Total transactions = 11,709

to explain the first of these phenomena, a small scale user survey was conducted at the University of Houston Libraries to determine if users were identifying items at other HARLiC libraries through the use of the CD-ROM union catalog and then visiting the libraries to use or obtain these materials. While some of the users que-

FIGURE 4

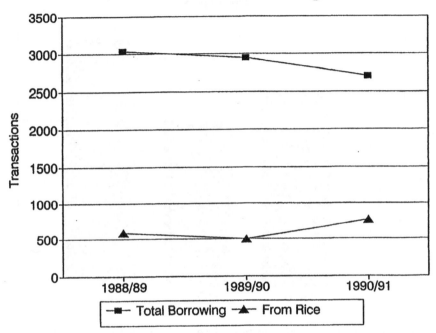

UH HARLiC ILL Borrowing

ried did indicate that the option described above was one that they intended to follow, at this time the sample is too small to provide reliable information. This study should be continued over a longer period of time in order to obtain useful data. Anecdotal evidence that indicates increased circulations to University of Houston students has been provided by Houston Public Library circulation staff. No statistics, however, have been compiled to support this perception.

ILL PROCEDURES

The HARLiC ILL borrowing statistics reflect the number of requests actually filled by the Consortium libraries. They do not show the number of requests actually sent to these libraries. Only

FIGURE 5

UH ILL Borrowing
from Rice

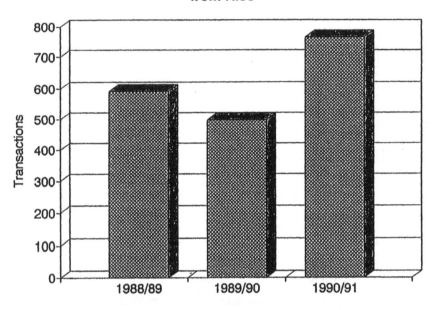

by counting the actual number of requests sent to each HARLiC participant over the last several years could an accurate comparison be made, and these statistics have not been compiled as of yet. It is possible that these figures might reveal an increase in the total number of HARLiC transactions.

The ILL Unit of the UH Libraries sends most of its requests via the OCLC ILL Subsystem. Requests are searched in the OCLC database for a matching bibliographic record, a workform is created for each request, and the requests are sent to a maximum of five lending libraries. If the first library on the lending string is unable to fill the request, for whatever reason, the request is automatically sent to the next library on the string.

The UH ILL Unit always selects as its first string of lending libraries the HARLiC libraries and the other UH System libraries (i.e., UH-Downtown, UH-Clear Lake, and UH-Victoria) displayed

FIGURE 6a

UH HARLiC ILL Borrowing
1988/89

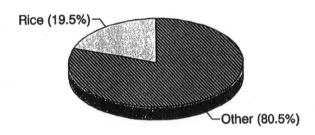

Rice (19.5%)

Other (80.5%)

Total transactions = 3,034

FIGURE 6b

UH HARLiC ILL Borrowing
1990/91 (projected)

Rice (28.4%)

Other (71.6%)

Total transactions = 2,694

as holders on the OCLC bibliographic record. After the HARLiC union catalog became available to UH patrons, ILL began receiving requests with HARLiC library holding information appearing in the source of citation line. In such instances, the ILL staff search the OCLC database for a bibliographic record that displays ownership

FIGURE 7

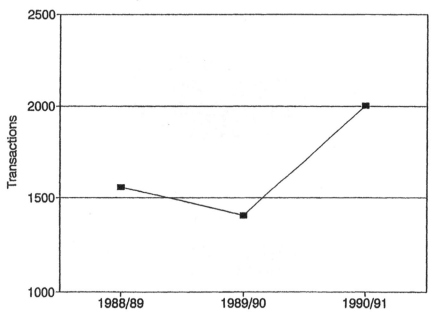

Borrowing from Rice
by other HARLiC Libraries

by a HARLiC library. Not all records or holdings information found in the HARLiC catalog are reflected in the OCLC database. If no OCLC bibliographic record is found that displays ownership by a HARLiC library, the OCLC library symbol for the HARLiC library (or libraries) displayed in the HARLiC catalog is included in the lending string of the ILL workform, along with its citation source in the VERIFIED field.

The number of filled ILL transactions between participating HARLiC libraries may not have increased with the implementation of the HARLiC Union Catalog, but UH patrons are certainly aware of the catalog and are using it to identify needed materials in the collections of participating HARLiC libraries. Before the availability of the HARLiC catalog, patrons filling out ILL requests usually

FIGURE 8

HARLiC ILL Activity

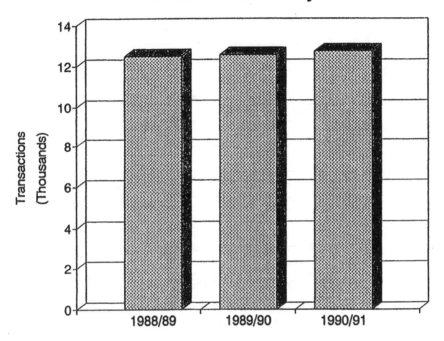

did not identify a HARLiC library source. Unless a reference/information staff member had searched the OCLC database, users generally did not have access to holdings information. Since the advent of the HARLiC catalog, users are able to identify the HARLiC library (libraries) owning the item and expect to receive the material from that source in a timely manner. To expedite the processing of such requests, one staff member is assigned the task of handling these requests on a rush basis.

One noticeable impact of the HARLiC catalog may not be so much in the increase of total ILL transactions among Consortium members, but rather in the increased awareness of patrons of the availability of needed materials at these other institutions and their resulting expectation of speedy document delivery. As a result, the

FIGURE 9

UH ILL Borrowing

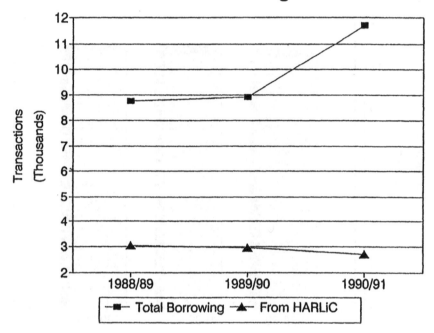

HARLiC libraries should focus their attention on improving processing time and guaranteeing efficient document delivery between member libraries.

PROPOSALS FOR ILL ENHANCEMENTS

In response to the increased user demands for faster turnaround time for ILL service between HARLiC libraries, it may be necessary for HARLiC members to reconsider the procedures used to process ILL transactions within the Consortium. Presently, all ILL requests submitted by HARLiC libraries to one another are transmitted via the OCLC ILL Subsystem as previously mentioned. At the University of Houston Libraries, OCLC ILL requests are automatically downloaded and printed at the end of each working day using the ILL Micro Enhancer program and are processed the next working day. Those items that the library has been able to retrieve are sent to the requesting HARLiC library via the HARLiC courier. Requests for journal articles require an extra day of processing time because the journals are sent to the Libraries' Copy Center for photocopying. The Copy Center returns these items to ILL for mailing.

One possible technique for improving turnaround time in the handling of ILL requests among HARLiC libraries would be to process those requests identified by the patrons as being owned by a HARLiC library on the day of receipt instead of waiting until the next work day. The time needed to fulfill the request would be improved by at least one day. Use of telefacsimile instead of the HARLiC courier would expedite further the fulfillment of journal article requests among the HARLiC libraries by cutting one to three days off the turnaround time.

Another method for even more rapid document delivery service of journal articles would be the implementation of Ariel(R),[3] a new document transmission system designed by the Research Libraries Group (Jackson 1991). Using a computer, document scanner, laser printer, Ariel software, and the Internet, documents of high print quality could be transmitted rapidly among the HARLiC libraries. The Internet transmission rate is significantly higher than a fax transmission speed of 9600 bps. With this system there is usually no need to photocopy documents before transmitting them; they can be scanned, in most instances, directly from the piece. In addition to eliminating the time and expense required for photocopying, Ariel eliminates the staff time spent in packaging, labeling, and mailing the items.

An alternative method to improve processing and document delivery time would be to establish a telecommunications link among the HARLiC libraries, along with the development of software to gather pertinent information from the bibliographic record and the patron and then send this request electronically to the holding library. This software must not only include the capabilities of creating and receiving requests, but must also be able to monitor request status, update requests, and provide statistical reports (Dutcher 1989). In cases where more than one HARLiC library owns an item, the capability to automatically route the request to the next library in the lending string would be highly desirable. Since the HARLiC catalog currently does not include summary holdings information for serials, it would be preferable to send only monographic requests on this system until summary holdings statements are added. Alternatively, Ariel, or a similar computer-based document delivery system, could be used to process photocopy requests after a search in the OCLC Union List Subsystem has verified ownership of the requested volume by a HARLiC library.

While waiting for a HARLiC interlibrary loan system to be designed that would allow the creation, routing, and updating of ILL requests among the various HARLiC libraries, the UH Libraries could develop a software package for internal use that would allow the user to capture pertinent data from the HARLiC bibliographic record, transfer this information automatically to an ILL request template, add necessary patron identification information, and print out the request for submission to ILL (or perhaps send it electronically over a network). ILL staff would then rush process all such requests.

Adoption of any of the above suggestions would expedite the handling of ILL transactions among the HARLiC libraries. Some methods would have greater impact than others, and some would entail greater costs. But one (or more) of these ideas should be evaluated, modified as necessary, and implemented by the Consortium in order to provide better service to users and to more fully exploit the potential benefits of the HARLiC union catalog.

CONCLUSION

At first glance, the conclusion seems to be that the introduction of the HARLiC union catalog has had no concrete impact on interlibrary borrowing among the libraries (based on extrapolations from the UH data). It is too early, however, to view such a conclusion as final. The hypotheses stated previously need to be re-examined within the next several years when the catalog is in greater use in all of the HARLiC libraries and when it contains records for all of the member libraries. As use of the catalog grows, it is also becoming apparent that the original hypotheses as to the probable impact of the union catalog were formulated too narrowly. In all likelihood, the experiences of the next several years will demonstrate that the most important effect of the catalog is not in increased statistics (or lack thereof), but in the changes that will occur in users' perceptions and expectations of what the library can do.

In turn, these changes in user attitudes will promote complementary changes in the Consortium's reciprocal borrowing and lending policies and procedures. Many of the libraries are located in relative proximity to one another (e.g., all of the HARLiC libraries in Houston are within a five-mile radius). To some extent, users affiliated with one institution already visit the other libraries when the need arises. As the union catalog becomes more readily available to the public throughout the HARLiC libraries, it is likely that the number of times users will visit a library, other than the one they primarily use to obtain materials, will increase. As HARLiC library users become more informed about the collections of other HARLiC libraries, they also may increase the number of requests for HARLiC ILL service.

Even though it is not possible to demonstrate in a quantifiable manner that the HARLiC union catalog has had an enormously positive effect on resource sharing among the member libraries as of yet, nevertheless, over time, the existence of such a comprehensive and powerful tool will increase the utility of the combined collections of the HARLiC libraries. Not only will the items in this "virtual library" be more accessible to all HARLiC library users and thus better used, but also the existence of the union catalog and the resulting interlibrary use patterns could facilitate increased cooperative collection development among HARLiC libraries. These developments will improve the Consortium's ability to meet users' needs, and to spend materials budgets more effectively.

NOTES

1. Rice University initially elected not to participate.
2. Data were examined for academic years 1988/89, 1989/90, and 1990/91. Data for 1990/91 have been projected based on actual HARLiC courier statistics

for September 1990-April 1991 or actual University of Houston ILL statistics for September 1990-May 1991.

3. Ariel is a registered trademark of the Research Libraries Group, Inc.

REFERENCES

Dutcher, Gale A. "DOCLINE: A National Automated Interlibrary Loan Request Routing and Referral System." *Information Technology and Libraries* 8 (1989): 359-370.

Jackson, Mary. "Ariel(R) Beta Tester's Report." *Operations Update* (The Research Libraries Group, Inc.) 57 (March 1991): 6-8.

The OCLC/AMIGOS
Collection Analysis CD:
A Unique Tool for Collection
Evaluation and Development

Albert H. Joy

SUMMARY. The OCLC/AMIGOS Collection Analysis CD (CA-CD) is a microcomputer-based tool for the evaluation and development of library collections.[1] Based on a ten-year subset of library monographic holdings reported to OCLC, the CACD produces many different statistical reports comparing the evaluating library's collection with peer groups of libraries. These include reports on collection count, gap, overlap, and uniqueness. The CACD also produces bibliographic lists based on these measures. This article describes the OCLC/AMIGOS Collection Analysis CD and gives examples of how this tool may be used.

INTRODUCTION

The OCLC/AMIGOS Collection Analysis CD (CACD) is a microcomputer-based tool for collection evaluation and development. The CACD was developed by OCLC, Inc. (the Online Library Computer Center) and is marketed and supported by the AMIGOS Bibliographic Council, Inc. The CACD enables the user or "evaluator" to compare his or her collection with preselected peer groupings of library collections. The system generates statistical reports and bibliographic lists that provide a broad overview of

Albert H. Joy is Collection Development Librarian at the University of Vermont.

© 1992 by The Haworth Press, Inc. All rights reserved.

23

the library's monograph collection as well as detailed title-by-title comparisons based on the Library of Congress (LC) classification schedule. Manipulating the systems parameters allows the user to conduct a series of what-if analyses to evaluate various acquisitions schemes. Results can be viewed on the computer screen, printed, or saved in a computer file for future use.

There are two caveats that need to be stated in the beginning. First, the CACD is a system that while easy to use is difficult to understand. The CACD is interesting in part because it is a unique tool for collection evaluation and development. This uniqueness, however, requires caution in its use. It is very important to understand what this tool is and what it is not! Second, the gathering and presenting of library statistics is a challenge to one and all. Library statistics are, on one hand, precise and, on the other hand, difficult to describe. With the statistics generated by the CACD as with all other library statistics it is imperative to give clear definition to the source of the data and to give care in its description to others.

HARDWARE AND SOFTWARE REQUIREMENTS

In order to present its data on a microcomputer workstation, the CACD is prepared on both floppy diskettes and on a compact disc. The producers of the system have specific hardware requirements. In practice, however, the CACD will work on a broad range of equipment. AMIGOS will lend a demonstration copy of the system to libraries that wish to check their specific workstation configurations.

THE DATABASE

The CACD database is issued once a year and contains a 10-year subset of the OCLC database. To be included in the subset the records must be monographic, include an LC (Library of Congress) or NLM (National Library of Medicine) class number, and held by at least one Association of Research Libraries (ARL) library. Serial records, government documents, and theses and dissertations are excluded. Because they are classified as state documents, state university press publications are also excluded. Vagaries in the cataloging of these materials is the basis for their exclusion. From a collection evaluation and development standpoint, this is unfortunate. The lack of serial records is especially felt. In the 1990's when many libraries are re-evaluating (i.e., cutting) their serial holdings, this information would be useful. Nevertheless, since OCLC records for serials, government documents, and theses are uneven, a reflection of current cataloging practice, their exclusion is understandable.

Libraries that use the Dewey Decimal Classification system will not be able to use this system. OCLC/AMIGOS decided to exclude Dewey and are not currently working on the problem, because of the difficulty deciding which version of Dewey to implement. The NLM component of the CACD is also of limited utility, because there are few medical school libraries represented in the database.

There are approximately 1.7 million abbreviated bibliographic records included on the compact disc. Each record contains author, title, publisher, year of publication, language, International Standard Book Number (ISBN), and OCLC number all taken from either the fixed or variable fields of the OCLC MARC (Machine Readable Cataloging) records. Truncation of this information may occur because only 100 characters display from MARC 1xx and 245 fields.

PEER GROUPS

Comparing the evaluator's holdings acquired in the last ten years to the holdings of various groups of libraries is the essence of the CACD. The basic product comes with fourteen peer groups. In addition, a user may define one to four additional peer groups. The basic peer groups are defined by size, ARL membership, academic degrees given, and graduate programs. The sizes are based on volume holdings counts reported to the American Library Directory (ALD) which is the most comprehensive source for library holdings.

The fourteen basic peer groups are divided into five categories: ARL libraries, libraries with between 700,000 and one million vol-

umes, libraries with between 300,000 and 700,000 volumes, libraries with between 100,000 and 300,000 volumes, and libraries with
between 50,000 and 100,000 volumes. The University of Vermont
Library primarily uses the peer group for libraries that report
700,000 to 999,999 volumes, its collection size at the time the
current CACD was issued. It can be useful to compare one's library to peer groups both bigger and smaller than one's own.

USER-DEFINED PEER GROUPS

User-defined peer groups give a library a chance to compare its
holdings against a specific group of libraries. The evaluator may,
for a price, create up to four user-defined peer groups. The groups
may contain between two and one hundred different OCLC holdings codes. If one wishes to create a peer group of one, to compare
holdings against just one library, the permission of that institution
is required, since the holdings of each library are considered confi-
dential. In the larger peer groups, it is not possible to select one
specific library with which to compare oneself.

There are many options for designing peer groups. Some colleges and universities have an institutional peer group with which they
regularly compare themselves. The peer grouping that the University of Vermont uses is based on an historical comparison of library
budgets as reported to the Association of College and Research
Libraries (ACRL). Correlating just the materials budget may be a
better method of comparison. Materials budgets are more closely
tied to holdings and are less affected by local impact on items such
as salary levels.

Regional peer groups are an option for some, though not all,
libraries. At the University of Vermont, a regional peer grouping
would not be practical due to great institutional difference and geographical distance. If conditions warrant, a peer group composed of
local or regional resource sharing libraries is a good choice. Institutions that sign resource sharing agreements allow users of one library in the group to use some or all of the resources of all libraries
in the group. The agreement may differ from group to group.

One must be honest and as precise as possible in using this product, although, given the nature of statistics, this process is difficult at best. It is important to describe fully the peer group used in the analysis. There can be several legitimate peer groups with which to compare a library–a user-defined peer group or a size-based one. The evaluator should prepare analyses using all defensible peer groups to identify the one that best meets the needs of the occasion. For example, a library facing accreditation or applying for a grant may select different peer groups than when compiling a budget request. In each case the numbers will be accurate and the peer group will genuinely reflect the selected method of describing the library.

SOFTWARE COMPONENTS

For performing its job of collection evaluation and development, the CACD has two major components: statistical tables, called Metrics, and Bibliographic Lists. Some projects will use the statistical tables solely (e.g., accreditation requests, grant support requests, and other projects in which the goal is descriptive in nature). Projects that are related to collection building will also use the bibliographic lists. The opening menus indicate the available options in the CACD (Figure 1).

Metrics

Both the collection metrics and subcollection metrics tables provide the same options. The collection metrics tables produce reports based on a thirty-two LC/NLM subject class division while the subcollection metrics tables produce reports based on the five hundred subject divisions of the National Shelflist 500 (NSL).[2]

The COUNTS report provides a table comparing, by LC division, the number of titles and aggregate holdings of the selected peer group with the number of titles in the evaluator's collection. This report also shows the number of unique titles held by only one peer group member. Finally, the amount of overlap between the evaluating library and other peer group members is shown.

The PROPORTIONS report provides three important pieces of information. In a table arranged by LC division, this report com-

FIGURE 1. CACD Opening Menus

Main Menu

```
C) Collection Metrics
S) Subcollection Metrics
B) Bibliographic Lists
D) Default Parameters
E) Exit to DOS
```

Collection Metrics Menu

```
C) Counts
P) Proportions
O) Overlap
H) Holdings Distribution
G) Gap
U) Uniqueness
```

Bibliographic Lists Menu

```
O) Overlap
G) Gap
U) Unique Evaluator
N) Unique Peer Group
E) Evaluator List
P) Peer Group List
```

pares the evaluator's title count to the title count of a statistically generated average peer group member. It calculates the mean total number of titles held by libraries in the peer group. The comparative size of the two figures is given, as well as the percentage that the specific LC division is of the total collection of both the evaluator and the peer group. Unfortunately, there is no option here, or in the other tables, to find the median figures which might account for collection extremes.

The OVERLAP report shows how titles and holdings in the evaluator's collection overlap with the selected peer group. It also shows percentage of overlap for both titles and holdings.

The HOLDINGS DISTRIBUTION report compares the evaluator's collection to the selected peer group based on holdings. This important table shows how many peer group members hold the titles that the evaluator holds. Therefore, the evaluator can see how many titles are held by all peer group members or other relative percentages of the peer group. This report can show if there is a core group of titles held by all libraries or if the majority of titles are held by only a few institutions.

The GAP report, like the Holdings Distribution report, compares the evaluator's collection to the peer group by holdings. This report, however, shows how many titles held by various groups of peer libraries are *not* held by the evaluator. This report also shows the relationship between selective collection building and the comparative size of the collection in the specific LC division.

The UNIQUENESS report compares counts of unique titles in the entire peer group, the evaluator's collection, and the collection of the statistically generated average peer group member.

Bibliographic Lists

The various options on the bibliographic lists menu (Figure 1) show the type of lists that can be generated. The descriptions of the metric reports apply here as well. Instead of producing statistical tables, however, these reports produce bibliographic lists. The Overlap List creates a list of bibliographic records that are held both by the evaluator and by selected members of the peer group. The Gap List indicates which titles are lacking in the collection. The two unique listings show titles held solely by the evaluator and by the peer groups. The final lists can show elements of or the total list of titles in the database. In all of these choices, the selection of default parameters are extremely useful in designing lists. Whether by the very specific LC class number, language, or date, a list can be developed that best meets the needs of the occasion.

CACD APPLICATIONS

The CACD is used to describe the library in comparison with various groups of libraries for many purposes, including accreditation, re-accreditation, and grant support; review of current and proposed collection levels; budget preparation; verification of collection development policy goals; and cooperative collection development.

Accreditation, Re-accreditation, and Grant Support

Most libraries are regularly called upon to provide information about their collections. The requests come from academic departments, programs, schools within the institution, and from the institution itself. The information is used to support a number of needs at the institution including accreditation and re-accreditation of programs, supporting grants, justifying new programs, and providing information for institutional statistical reporting. The CACD can be used for a number of these requests, but it will not be useful for all. The CACD compares only a ten-year subset of monographic holdings. Since the ARL, ACRL, and ALD questionnaires request information on the complete holdings of libraries, the CACD would not be of use for them.

Requests for accreditation and re-accreditation can be very specific. For example, the following two re-accreditations were processed this past year at the University of Vermont: the ABET (Accreditation Board for Engineering and Technology) and the AACSB (American Assembly of Collegiate Schools of Business). The ABET has very specific needs. The library was asked to produce holdings information and expenditure figures for the previous three fiscal years. With the CACD it is not possible to account for monographic series or serials. The second re-accreditation, the AACSB, required specific information like the ABET. At first glance, there seemed to be no role for the CACD. The Library Faculty Liaison to the Business School and the Collection Development Librarian, however, decided to add data generated by the CACD as supplementary information. This information was well received by the Business School and was incorporated into the official packet of information used in responding to the AACSB re-accreditation.

The information supplied to the Business School included two graphs developed with data from the CACD (Figures 2, 3). The library also provided the peer group list which had been annotated to show which peer group members offered MBA programs. The CACD does not include a graphing module, but data from the CACD is tabular in format, and can be imported easily into a database or a spreadsheet program.

Figure 2 is simplistic in design, but it served its purpose well as part of the package supporting the University of Vermont's Business School. While it is accurate, it is not very informative beyond a rough description of the University of Vermont Libraries collection strengths and weaknesses.

FIGURE 2

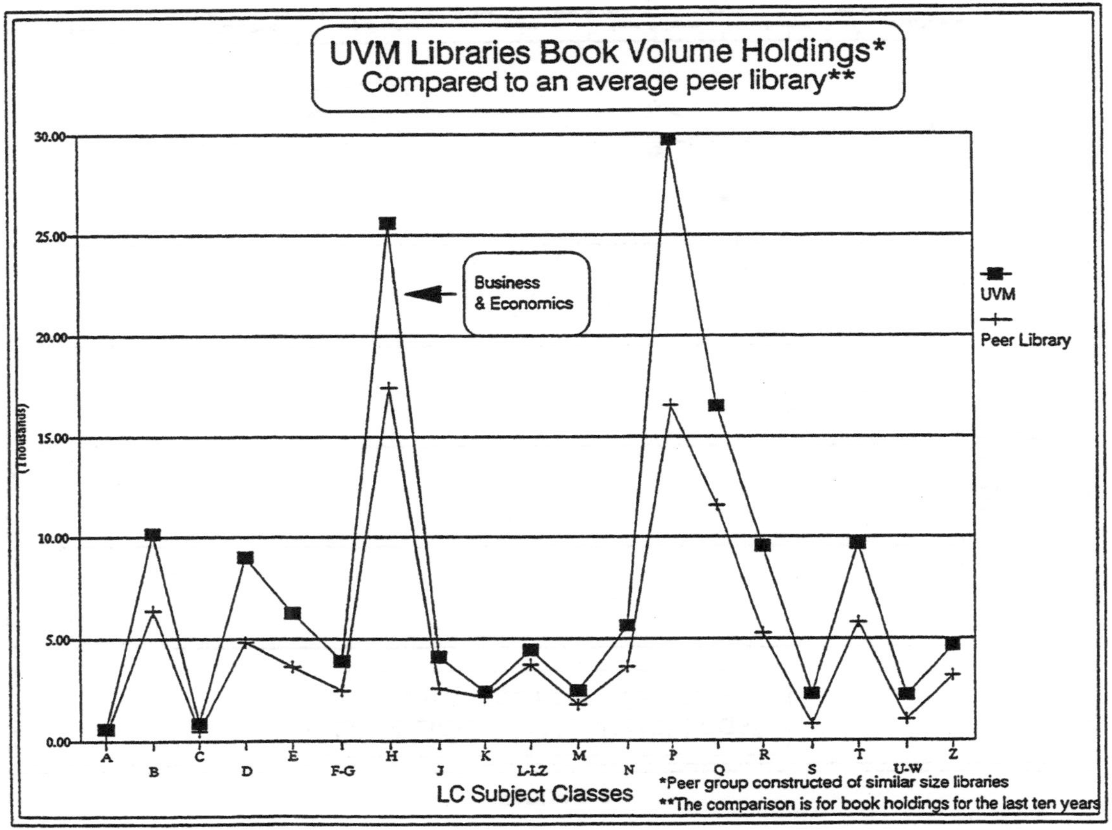
UVM Libraries Book Volume Holdings*
Compared to an average peer library**
30.00
25.00
20.00
15.00
10.00
5.00
0.00
(Thousands)
Business
& Economics
UVM
Peer Library
A
B
C
D
E
F-G
H
J
K
L-LZ
M
N
P
Q
R
S
T
U-W
Z
LC Subject Classes
*Peer group constructed of similar size libraries
**The comparison is for book holdings for the last ten years

FIGURE 3

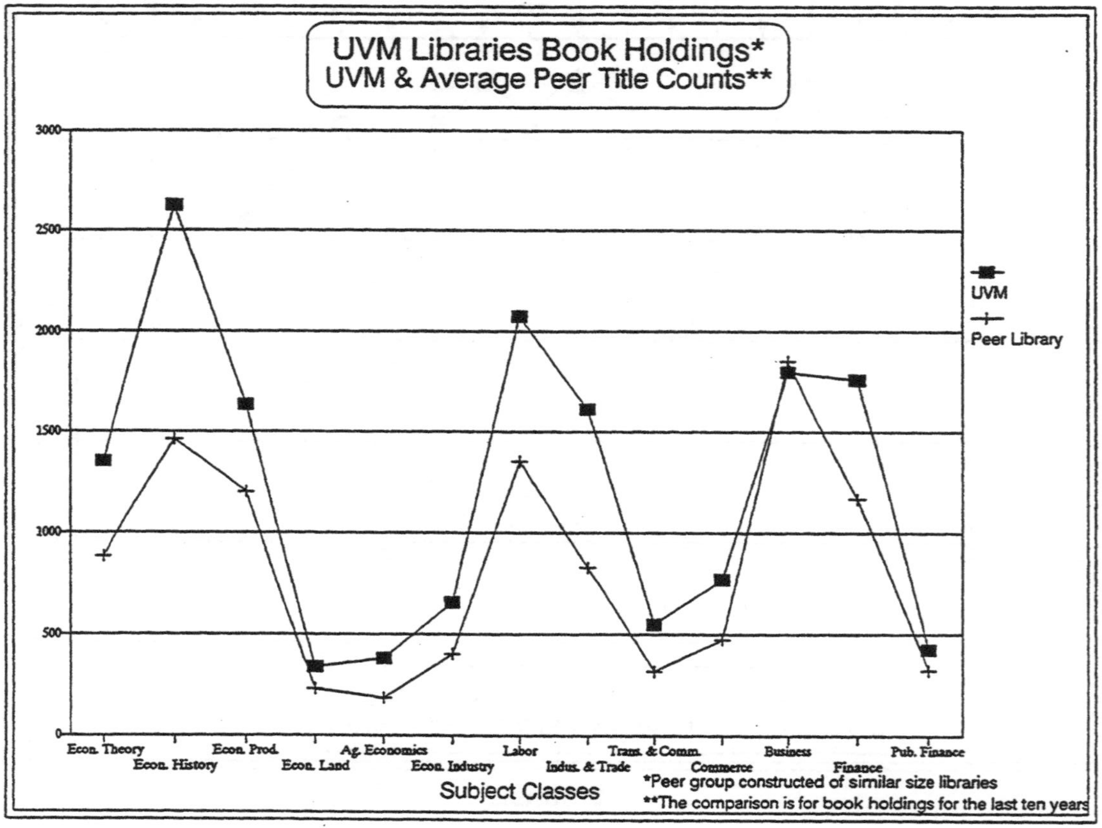

UVM Libraries Book Holdings*
UVM & Average Peer Title Counts**

■ UVM
+ Peer Library

*Peer group constructed of similar size libraries
**The comparison is for book holdings for the last ten years

Subject Classes

Econ. Theory   Econ. Prod.   Ag. Economics   Labor   Indus. & Trade   Trans. & Comm.   Commerce   Business   Finance   Pub. Finance
Econ. History   Econ. Land   Econ. Industry

32

Although the CACD is a useful tool for providing information on certain accreditation requests, it is only a small subset of the total holdings of a library. As such, its utility is limited to a supporting role, and users should explain these limitations for data generated for these purposes. Care must be exercised in selecting the peer group for an accreditation project as well. Peer group members should have similar academic programs (e.g., MBA programs, Engineering programs, etc.). The library might even choose to add one or more user-defined peer groups based on major upcoming re-accreditation projects.

Review of Current Collection Levels and Budget Planning

The identification of a weak area of the collection is not always followed by a collection building project. Further evaluation is necessary to justify such a project. The AACSB re-accreditation described previously is the source for the following examples. During the evaluation of the business collection for the AACSB, one NSL 500 division was of concern. The graphs in Figures 3 and 4 were produced at the same time. The first was included in the package sent to the Business School, the second was not.

Along the X-Axis at the bottom are the National Shelflist 500 divisions for Economics and Business. In Figure 3, the graph lines illustrate the University of Vermont's title counts for these divisions and the statistically generated average peer group member's title count. The University of Vermont has consistently more titles than the average peer group member with one exception, HF5001–HF6351–the specific heading called Business.

The graph in Figure 4 illustrates this even better. The basis for this graph is relationship of the University of Vermont's title count to that of the average peer group member. The University of Vermont title count was divided by the average member title count. This identification of an apparently weak area of the collection is one of the strengths of the CACD. These data were developed using the CACD for 1978-1988. The tables in Figures 5 and 6 were downloaded from the 1979-1989 edition of the CACD. They indicate how the CACD helps to determine the correct response to the problem.

FIGURE 4

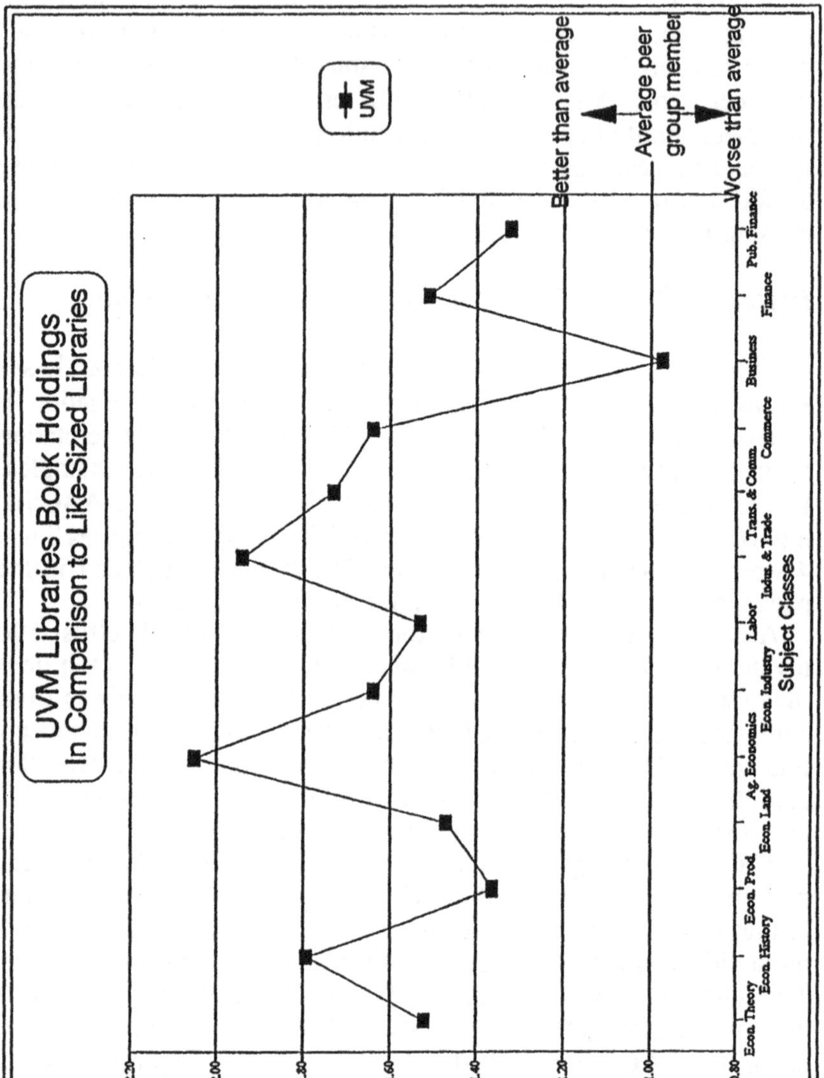

UVM Libraries Book Holdings
In Comparison to Like-Sized Libraries
UVM
Better than average
Average peer group member
Worse than average
2.20
2.00
1.80
1.60
1.40
1.20
1.00
0.80
Econ. Theory
Econ. History
Econ. Prod.
Econ. Land
Ag. Economics
Econ. Industry
Labor
Indus. & Trade
Trans. & Comm.
Commerce
Business
Finance
Pub. Finance
Subject Classes

FIGURE 5. Subcollection Holdings Table

Subcollection Holdings Distribution
Peer Group: VTU User Defined Peer Group 1 (46)

Division		Holdings Range	Titles			Pct of Evaluator to	
			Eval-uator	Peer Group	Average Member	Peer	Avg Mbr
HF5001-HF6351		90-100%	11	11	10	100.0	107.7
Business		80-89%	104	122	102	85.2	101.7
		70-79%	139	200	149	69.5	93.2
Current:		60-69%	221	361	234	61.2	94.4
Peer Holdings	103,610	50-59%	213	369	204	57.7	104.5
Overlap Holdings	34,800	40-49%	259	657	298	39.4	86.8
VTU Titles	1,755	30-39%	244	1,003	343	24.3	71.1
Comparative Size	77.92%	20-29%	197	1,180	291	16.7	67.7
		10-19%	220	2,501	370	8.8	59.4
		1-09%	124	3,126	188	4.0	66.0
		Unique	23	2,846	62	0.8	37.2
Total		0-100%	1,755	12,376	2,252	14.0	77.9

FIGURE 6. Subcollection Gap Table

Subcollection Gap
Peer Group: VTU User Defined Peer Group 1 (46)

Division		Holdings Range	Gap titles		Comparative Size
			In Range	Cumulative	
HF5001-HF6351		90-100%	0	0	77.92%
Business		80-89%	18	18	78.72%
		70-79%	61	79	80.63%
Current:		60-69%	140	219	84.13%
VTU Titles	1,755	50-59%	156	375	84.84%
Comparative Size	77.92%	40-49%	398	773	95.59%
		30-39%	759	1,532	111.61%
		20-29%	983	2,515	121.56%
		10-19%	2,281	4,796	179.19%
		1-09%	3,002	7,798	211.20%
		Unique	2,846	10,644	204.27%
Total		0-100%	10,644	10,644	550.48%

The Subcollection Holdings Distribution Table (Figure 5) shows how the titles in this division are held among the peer group. It shows that 10,656 of the 12,376 titles, or 86% of the titles, are held by between 1% and 40% of the forty-six peer group members (i.e., between one and eighteen libraries). Only 14% of the titles are held in common by a large group of peer group members. The University of Vermont is faced with a choice: to build a collection of commonly held items or to build a collection of more rarely held titles. To build a comprehensive collection, a library would proba- bly select not only the widely held items, but also the rarely held items.

These statistics indicate that the University of Vermont is weakest in rarely held materials, those titles held by only 1% to 50% of the peer group (i.e., between one and twenty-three libraries). The University of Vermont is not weak in the commonly held items, those items held by 50% to 100% of the peer group (i.e., between twenty-three and forty-six libraries). In this category, the University of Vermont has 98% of the holdings of the average peer group member.[3] Figure 6 suggests various strategies for resolving this problem.

The Subcollection Gap Table (Figure 6) shows the holdings of the peer group in relation to those titles that the evaluator does not have. It also shows the result of different collection building strategies. For instance, if the University of Vermont decided to add books that 60% to 69% of the forty-six peer libraries hold (140 additional books), the comparative size of the University of Vermont's collection would rise from 77.92% to 84.13%, an increase of slightly over 6%. If the University of Vermont wanted to raise its comparative size over a few years, perhaps 10% a year, this table would be useful for developing a plan to present to the administration.

In this scenario, suppose that the University of Vermont would add 219 additional titles (i.e., the cumulative titles held by 60% to 100% of the peer group that the University of Vermont does not currently hold). The comparative size then would rise to 87.66% of the average member,[4] an increase of approximately 10%. The average price for books in this category based on the Blackwell North American report for FY89 is $37.28. Therefore, to begin to correct the collection weakness by approximately 10% per year for two to three years, an additional $8,164 would have to be spent each year.

As discussed previously, the analysis of the Holdings Distribution Table (Figure 5) indicated that the gap in the University of Vermont collection is not in those titles commonly held, but in the rarely held ones. If the goal is to add titles so that the University of Vermont collection count is equal to that of the average peer group member, the collection building should occur in those more rarely held titles. Figure 7 shows the difference between the holdings of the University of Vermont and that of the average peer group member.[5] These data represent the number of books that need to be added to match the average collection. The total collection building project should cost approximately $15,700, using the average price of $37.28.

FIGURE 7. Comparison of UVM to Average Peer

Holdings Distribution	Gap
40-49%	39
30-39%	99
20-29%	94
10-19%	150
Unique	39
TOTAL	421

There are many caveats with this approach. Obviously the average price of materials has been steadily increasing. The 1989 Blackwell report was used because the current CACD database covers 1979-1989. This approach assumes the existence of a retrospective buying plan to attempt to purchase materials that the University of Vermont missed during the past few years. To attempt to purchase materials more than a few years old would be difficult, if not impossible, since materials go out of print after only a few years. Of course, not all materials on the gap list would be desirable for the University of Vermont collection. But the target figures in this table give leeway for informed selection. The table in Figure 7 was developed by the author and is not part of the CACD. It provides valid information for those following the scenario previously described, and it could be incorporated into the existing Subcollection Gap report.

A careful review of the bibliographic list (Figure 8) is necessary to match acquisitions to the collection profile. For instance, the University of Vermont rarely acquires business books in languages other than English. Also, the University of Vermont does not acquire guidebooks except by specific faculty request. The list also needs to be compared with the online catalog to identify cases where the book is owned but in another edition. The titles in the Business range that the University of Vermont does not have will be reviewed for possible acquisition.

There is a serendipitous benefit to be derived from the biblio-

FIGURE 8. Sample Bibliographic List

```
Ethics in practice managing the moral corporation edited, with an
introduction by Kenneth R.
Harvard Business School Press, 1989
OCLC = 18816226   ISBN = 0875842070


Mathews, M. Cash.
Strategic intervention in organizations resolving ethical dilemmas
M. Cash M
Sage Publications, 1988
OCLC = 17918638   ISBN = 0803933037


Papers on the ethics of administration edited by N. Dale Wright.
Brigham Young University ;, 1988
OCLC = 18049746   ISBN = 0887069614


Robin, Donald P.
Business ethics where profits meet value systems Donald P. Robin,
R. Eric Rei
Prentice Hall, 1989
OCLC = 18557828   ISBN = 0130956392


AMA Winter Educators
1987 AMA Winter Educators' Conference marketing theory edited by
Russel W
American Marketing Association, 1987
OCLC = 15222915   ISBN = 0877571856


Heller, Robert, 1932
The supermarketers marketing for success, rules of the master
marketers, th
Dutton, 1987
OCLC = 14270701   ISBN = 0525245200


Levitt, Theodore, 19
The marketing imagination Theodore Levitt.
Free Press ;, 1986
OCLC = 13420503   ISBN = 0029191807
```

graphic lists resulting from gaps in a collection. Many of these books should have come on one of the University of Vermont's approval plans. For instance, the University of Vermont has an approval plan to acquire U.S. trade press and university press publications. Business materials are included in the approval plan profile and should come under the plan. In analyzing the presses from the gap list, at least one press was identified that was missing from the approval plan press list.

As mentioned previously, the approval plans exclude guidebooks. This study will provide the opportunity to review this exclusion in general and for business materials in particular. It is possible that guidebooks form a larger percentage of the material in this class range. Knowing that fact, the University of Vermont can choose to maintain the current collection policies if determined best for the collection and mission to support the university curriculum.

In sum, analyzing the business collection produced several interesting outcomes. In addition to providing material that the Business School could use in their re-accreditation project, it helped to identify a weak area of the collection and a potentially weak spot in the collection development plan. Finally, the lists and tables provided strategies to correct the problem over a reasonable time period.

Verification of Collection Development Policy Goals

There are many ways for the CACD to be used to verify collection development policy goals. The following are two examples. The first example shows how the CACD can identify an area that has possibly received more funding than justified by the collection development policy. The second shows how the CACD can verify that a collection area is of appropriate size and how it can be used to respond to changes in policy.

The University of Vermont offers an M.A. program in German. The collection development policy states that the University supports master's programs at the 2a Advanced Study Level, as defined in *Guidelines for Collection Development* (Perkins 1979, 35). The data in Figure 9 indicate that the University of Vermont has a superlative German collection, at least in terms of comparative counts. In addition, this table represents a comparison of the University of Vermont to a peer group one level above its usual peer group of libraries holding 700,000 to 999,999 volumes.

This fact suggests two responses: self-congratulations for an impressive collection in the area of German Literature, or a re-evaluation of current collection levels. As with all conclusions about the specific findings of collection evaluation, care must be exercised in interpreting the results. In the case of German, the CACD evaluation has shown that the University of Vermont has many more titles than the average peer group member. Each test, however, is but one piece of the puzzle. Further evaluation of the collection is necessary to determine appropriate action. The graph in Figure 10 illustrates that the answer is not as easy as it may seem.

FIGURE 9. Subcollection Proportions Table

Subcollection Proportions
Peer Group: Large Academic Libraries > 1,000,000 (37)
LC Division: PT Literature: Germanic

NSL 500	------ Titles ------ Evaluator	Avg Mbr	Comparative Size	- Pct of Subcollection - Peer Group	Evaluator
PT1-PT0951	599	170	352.35	16.54	18.23
PT1100-PT148	93	21	442.86	2.06	2.83
PT1501-PT169	85	26	326.92	2.49	2.59
PT1701-PT179	26	7	371.43	0.70	0.79
PT1799-PT259	630	164	384.15	15.98	19.17
PT2600-PT265	974	342	284.80	33.32	29.64
PT2660-PT268	595	172	345.93	16.72	18.11
PT3701-PT489	125	35	357.14	3.45	3.80

Comparing the actual title counts shows that there are only four areas where the University of Vermont's collection is significantly above that of the average peer group member: German Literature–History and Criticism, German Literature–1700-1860, German Literature–1860-1960, and German Literature–1961-. In the other NSL divisions the proportions may be large but the actual title count difference is not significant. What should be done about the situation? In these days of strapped resources and serials cuts, this is a collection to be proud of and not one to curtail. It is not inappropriate for a program that offers an M.A. degree.

On the other end of the spectrum, analysis by the CACD has shown that the PZ5-10 National Shelflist range for children's literature is one of the weakest parts of the University of Vermont's collections. That is as it should be, because the University of Vermont was not collecting in this area. In fact, these data demonstrate correct selection efforts in the past to administrators reviewing collection development polices at the University of Vermont.

In 1989, a decision was made to change the collection policy to begin a vigorous collection program in this area. To assist the new collecting process, a bibliographic list of some of the missing titles was given to the librarian responsible for selecting children's literature. Succeeding editions of the CACD should reveal this intensi-

FIGURE 10

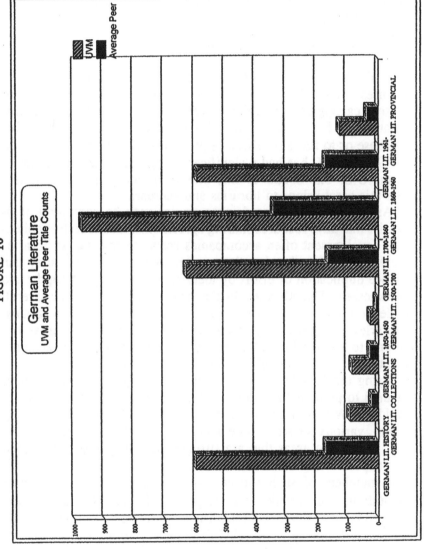

German Literature
UVM and Average Peer Title Counts

41

fied collecting. A similar adjustment to collection building in business is planned based on the CACD. Subsequent data will be shown to administrators as an example of the outcome of collection development policies.

Cooperative Collection Development

In the broadest sense of the term, resource sharing touches all the uses of the CACD. The resource being shared here is the cooperative cataloging effort that developed the OCLC bibliographic database. It is too easy to take for granted the great boon of this database or to focus on OCLC's problems. But, since its inception in 1972, OCLC has had a significant impact on academic libraries in the U.S. The CACD is only one of the many information uses that this asset brings to libraries and scholars.

As previously discussed, peer groups may be composed of libraries that have resource sharing agreements. Collaborative collection development often accompanies resource sharing. If libraries band together to develop their collections as a whole, they can reduce duplication of effort by identifying collection strengths and weaknesses. The libraries in the group can develop the overall collection by building on respective existing strong programs. Libraries can justify lower collection levels for those areas not central to the mission of the library and institution. These arrangements save some, though not all, duplication of effort.

Using the CACD for a resource sharing group is an excellent method to prepare for and to evaluate such cooperative collection building. With a peer group constructed of the resource sharing group, various reports can be generated analyzing collection overlap, identifying areas that are stronger than they should be based on cooperative agreements, and identifying areas neglected by all. The members of such a peer group need not be from separate institutions. Universities with large branch libraries can also use this model to evaluate and establish cooperative collection development.[6] Unfortunately, the CACD is limited to a narrow range of time and format. Much of the savings associated with resource sharing encompasses serial subscriptions and local and remote electronic sources of information. The CACD, however, can be used successfully for similar analyses of other types of library information.

The amount of unique items at the University of Vermont has been a striking discovery, one directly attributable to the CACD. A collection holding more than 80% of the total universe of titles in a given subject area is rare. Weeding and preserving these collections, therefore, must continue to be viewed with care. Further research is warranted.

CONCLUSION

The OCLC/AMIGOS Collection Analysis CD is a unique tool for the evaluation and development of library collections. Constructed as a subset of the titles and holdings reported to OCLC, the CACD helps libraries compare their collections to those of various peer groupings. Statistical tables aid in the description of existing collections and suggest ways to build or manage them.

Even though it is easy to use, the CACD presents several challenges. It is a narrow subset (if 1.7 million bibliographic records can be called narrow) of the massive OCLC database. Given its limitation to ten years of monographic records, one can question the relative importance of such a database in areas that rely heavily on journal literature (e.g., the sciences). Based on the Library of Congress classification system, the CACD provides broad and narrow subject analyses. Unfortunately, Dewey-based collections are excluded. Also excluded are analyses of cross-disciplinary programs such as women's studies and area studies.

Despite its limitations, however, the CACD does provide in-depth and thought-provoking collection evaluations. Additionally, it offers suggestions for collection building. The evaluator can follow a scenario from definition, to the application of relevant analyses, to its conclusion resulting in a list of books that are candidates for acquisition by the library. All of this from a microcomputer equipped simply with a hard disk and a CD-ROM drive. Currently in its third year, the OCLC/AMIGOS Collection Analysis CD is a program worthy of use and further investigation.

NOTES

1. For more information on the CACD contact the AMIGOS Bibliographic Council, Inc., 12200 Park Central Drive, Suite 500, Dallas, Texas 75251 (800)-843-8482 or Collette Mak, Marketing and User Services Division, OCLC, 6565 Frantz Road, Dublin, Ohio 43017-0702, (614)761-5053.

2. The NSL is maintained by the American Library Association, Association for Library Collections and Technical Services, Collection Management and Development Section, National Shelflist Count Committee.

3. This percentage is calculated by summing the values in the first five rows of column 2 (Evaluator) and column 4 (Average Member) in figure 5 and dividing the sum of column 2 data by the sum of column 4 data.

4. This percentage is calculated according to the following format: 1755 (current UVM holdings) + 219 (new titles) = 1974; 1974 (new UVM total)/ 2252 (average member holdings) = .8766.

5. These data are derived by subtracting the values in column 2 (Evaluator) from the values in column 4 (Average Member) of figure 5.

6. For more information on collection analysis and resource sharing see Kacena, Carolyn et al. "Collection Analysis and Resource Sharing: The OCLC/AMIGOS Collection Analysis System and the SMU Experience." In *Advances in Resource Sharing*, vol. 1, edited by Jennifer Cargill and Dianne J. Graves, 127-140. Westport, Conn.: Meckler Publishing, 1990.

SUGGESTED READING

Armbrister, Ann. "Library MARC Tapes as a Resource for Collection Analysis: The AMIGOS Service." In *Advances in Library Automation and Networking*, vol. 2, edited by Joe Hewitt, 119-135. Greenwich, Conn.: JAI Press, 1988.

Dillon, Martin. "Collection Analysis CD: A New Approach to Collection Assessment." *Library Hi Tech News* 65 (1989): 3-5.

Dillon, Martin et al. "Design Issues for a Microcomputer-based Collection Analysis System." *Microcomputers for Information Management* 5 (1988): 263-73.

Evans, G. T., R. Gifford, and D. R. Franz. *Collection Development Using OCLC Archival Tapes*. Washington, D.C.: U.S. Office of Education, Office of Libraries and Learning Resources, 1977. ERIC Document 152-299.

Kim, David U. "OCLC-MARC Tapes and Collection Management." *Information Technology and Libraries* 1 (March 1982): 22-27.

Kreyche, Michael. "BCL3 and NOTIS: An Automated Collection Analysis Project." *Library Acquisitions: Practice and Theory* 13 (1989): 323-328.

Moore, Barbara, Tamara J. Miller, and Don L. Tolliver. "Title Overlap: A Study of Duplication in the University of Wisconsin System Libraries." *College and Research Libraries* 43 (1982): 14-21.

Nisonger, Thomas E. "Editing the RLG Conspectus to Analyze the OCLC Archival Tapes of Seventeen Texas Libraries." *Library Resources and Technical Services* 29 (October/December 1985): 309-327.

Payson, Evelyn and Barbara Moore. "Statistical Collection Management Analysis of OCLC-MARC Tape Records." *Information Technology and Libraries* 3 (1985): 220-232.

Perkins, David L., ed. *Guidelines for Collection Development.* Chicago: American Library Association, 1979.

Reed-Scott, Jutta. "Information Technologies and Collection Development." *Collection Building* 3 (1989): 47-51.

Sanders, Nancy P., Edward T. O'Neill, and Stuart L. Weibel. "Automated Collection Analysis Using the OCLC and RLG Bibliographic Databases." *College and Research Libraries* 49 (1988): 305-314.

Vassallo, Benita Weber. "OCLC/AMIGOS Collection Analysis CD." *Against the Grain* 2 (1990): 30-31.

Social Science Perspectives
on Cooperative Collection Development

Charles A. Schwartz

SUMMARY. The model of "Combined Self-Interest," often invoked in discussions on the need for cooperative collection development consortia, has a number of broad, rather unrealistic assumptions about the way that the collection development process actually works. That model is reassessed from the perspective of certain social science models of a loosely-coupled system, which is characterized by ambiguous goals, problematic preferences, and hazy technology. The analysis provides an overview of the rapid institutionalization of the concept of cooperative collection development in the late 1970s, as well as a discussion of the differential prospects for tightening up cooperative collection consortia with respect to academic versus special libraries, science versus social science literatures, and serial versus book formats.

In theory, cooperative collection development is a fairly simple proposition that makes common sense. The standard model is that of "Combined Self-Interest," set forth in "A Guide to Coordinated and Cooperative Collection Development" by the Resources and Technical Services Division of the American Library Association in 1983 (Mosher and Pankake). Dougherty restates that model:

> If enough libraries would combine with major research libraries–and if each library could state specific needs for its own core collection based on the library's strengths, weaknesses,

Charles A. Schwartz is Social Sciences Librarian in the Fondren Library at Rice University, Houston, TX 77251-1892. He holds a PhD in Foreign Affairs from the University of Virginia and an MLS from Indiana University.

© 1992 by The Haworth Press, Inc. All rights reserved.

and special local conditions–a rational, coordinated pattern of collection development could be created to satisfy all participants' self-interest. (1988, 289)

The problem with that model, however, is that its main assumptions, or optimal conditions, are rarely found in practice. One condition is collection development goals that can be set definitively. Another is ready ability to coordinate selection choices between institutions. A third is adequate technology to evaluate and compare collections in an expedient fashion. Given the lack of such conditions, clearly apparent in the social sciences and humanities, it is not surprising that cooperative collection development consortia tend to exist only on the margins of academic programs.

This dichotomy between theory and practice underlies the analysis of cooperative collection development presented here. The analysis falls into three parts. The first one reviews the rapid transformation of cooperative collection development from a relatively minor concern during the first three-quarters of this century to an institutionalized concept about "the way things should be done." The second provides a broad interpretation of cooperative collection development from the perspective of certain social science models of a loosely-coupled system, which is characterized by ambiguous goals, problematic preferences, and hazy technology. The last part of the paper is in the nature of an overview; it describes conditions of successful cooperative collection development, distinguishing between loosely-coupled and tightly-coupled systems, and suggests some topics for future research.

INSTITUTIONALIZATION OF THE CONCEPT

Cooperative collection development as any sort of movement was born of disconcerting experiences with European acquisitions during and immediately after the Second World War. A number of large-scale programs were established to coordinate the collection and preservation of highly specialized research materials, usually of foreign origin. Principal programs included the Cooperative Acquisitions Project for Wartime Publications, conducted by the

Library of Congress in 1946; the Farmington Plan of designated responsibilities among sixty libraries for the acquisition of different countries' scholarly literature from 1948 to 1972; and the Center for Research Libraries, first established as a midwestern consortium in 1951.

Despite the important purpose they served, those programs had relatively little impact on conventional thinking about collection management until the mid-1970s. They were considered laudable departures from traditional institutional provincialism, but not as models to be emulated by less prestigious universities. There was little sense of an economic need for cooperative collection development in the library field as a whole.

While there were signs of change in the early 1970s–chiefly, the formation of the Research Libraries Group (RLG) in 1972 and a call for creation of medical library consortia in 1974 (Jones 1974), the idea of cooperative collection development had hardly been institutionalized in theory or practice. Indeed, an historical account of library cooperation published in 1975 noted a lack of "intellectual innovations" to motivate resource sharing (Stuart-Stubbs 1975, 662); and another account published at that time, also finding "little novelty" in incentives to cooperation over the past century, suggested that any real movement would take fifteen years–until the early 1990s–when a national online system would be in place (Weber 1976, 219).

Yet, within a few years cooperative collection development programs became a widespread phenomenon within the Association of Research Libraries (ARL). Whereas only seventeen programs among large university libraries had been established up to 1972, fifty-three new programs comprising at least one ARL member were established in the period from 1975 to 1983. In all, 80% of ARL institutions became members of collection development consortia or were actively planning to do so. Of those ARL institutions not yet involved, all reported in a survey that they were favorably disposed to the concept of cooperative collection development but perceived a lack of suitable partners (Hewitt and Shipman 1987, 202).

The pivotal year was 1976. In numbers alone, twelve programs–the most in any year–were begun. In terms of its conceptual advancement, cooperative collection development seems to be closely associated with White's (1976; 1980) studies at that time on the impact of inflation in scholarly publishing on libraries. Interestingly, White noted in a follow-up survey that 1976 was the first year in which libraries began to take cooperative collection development arrangements into account when considering serial cancellations (1981, 30).

It is not possible to ascertain from library science sources how collection development consortia have actually fared over the past decade. The literature in this area is largely descriptive and uncritical. Regional groups and local agreements are announced in library journals, but there are very few reports on the complexity or outcome of particular ventures. Most of what is known in any detail about the organizational experience of collection development programs is contained in a 1983 survey of ARL institutions by Hewitt and Shipman (1987).

That survey showed that most of the programs were still in the beginning stage of fostering organizational relationships. They had not reached the point where specific collection goals or responsibilities had been determined. If one takes into account the relatively recent dates when these programs had been created, this lag in momentum would seem natural. For example, a U.S. Office of Education survey in 1970 found that even technical kinds of library cooperative activities (e.g., interlibrary loan, union lists, document delivery) often took many years to put into operation (Cuadra 1972, 282).

Hewitt and Shipman discovered, however, that a basic, ongoing deterrent to cooperative collection development was the lack of comparable structure in collection management among member institutions:

> For example, one library relies principally on faculty selection, the other on bibliographer selection. Another library has a centralized collection development organization, the other a decentralized one. There is no direct correspondence of specialties among bibliographers. Problems were also reported with respect to selection guidelines and methods under cooperative agreements, the practical arrangements for making joint

purchase decisions, and the deficiencies of collection analysis tools for dividing collecting responsibilities in a practical way. (1987, 223)

Overall, many of the cooperative programs in 1983 appeared to be more passive than active in that they continued to rely heavily on traditional local patterns of collection development.

Although the Hewitt-Shipman survey is nearly a decade old, the situation it described so closely fits social science models of a loosely-coupled system that, by drawing on such models, it should be possible to make some reasonable inferences about contemporary problems and prospects for cooperative collection development in academic libraries.

LOOSE COUPLING IN COOPERATIVE COLLECTION DEVELOPMENT

The concept of loose coupling generally refers to incoherence and disjuncture between organizational means and ends. Writers use it to describe a number of organizational properties found in educational institutions, publishing houses, governmental bodies, multinational firms, military bureaucracies, and research units (Weick 1976; Cohen, March, and Olsen 1972; Lutz 1982; Schwartz 1989). Four properties of a loosely-coupled system apply to cooperative collection development programs.

1. *Open-ended goals,* such as "collecting at a research level." As Hewitt and Shipman found, cooperative collection development consortia tend to get stymied when attempting to make the transition from general problems to specific issues and concrete measures:

> Cooperative collection development was viewed by a number of respondents as a topic which lends itself all too well to rhetorical treatment. It seemed particularly resistant to systematic, decision-oriented approaches. A rather strong sense of frustration was expressed about the difficulty of focusing on issues that held some potentiality for practical outcomes. (1987, 200)

2. *Problematic preferences* for library acquisitions, owing to the extraordinary growth and inflation of scholarly materials and to the broad question of their intellectual quality.

3. *Relatively independent streams of problems* looking for situations in which they might be aired, as well as choices looking for opportunities, so that there is no definite organizational purpose or direction. Thus, Hewitt and Shipman reported abandoning an early attempt to categorize cooperative collection development activities:

> As the survey progressed, it became increasingly clear that most cooperative collection development programs are so broad in scope and so tied to an infinitely complex matrix of individual [interests], institutional collections, or inter-institutional patterns that they did not really fall into any specific predefined category or set of categories. (1987, 213)

This initial view was confirmed by the library respondents' general inability to specify the purpose or aims of their respective programs.

4. *Hazy technology* to evaluate collections and compare them across institutions. Three tools have been devised for this purpose: (a) the national shelflist measurement project, (b) the RLG Conspectus, and (c) the OCLC/AMIGOS Collection Analysis Compact Disc (CACD).

National Shelflist Measurement Project

The first shelflist count was conducted by seventeen research libraries in 1973; the last count, in 1985, involved forty-eight libraries, including the Library of Congress. This measure provides an approximation of cataloged titles held by each participating institution in as many as 490 Library of Congress subject ranges. Whether such quantitative data create false impressions about collection quality is a classic question. Some consensus exists that the national shelflist procedure is too time-consuming, and the data too cumbersome, to afford an adequate basis for setting specific cooperative collection goals or responsibilities (Branin, Farrell, and Tiblin 1985; Dannelly 1985).

RLG Conspectus

The RLG Conspectus offers a primarily qualitative approach to collection evaluation and coordination among large research libraries. It was originally envisioned in 1980 as a "new Farmington Plan," something like a national collection development policy to support foreign area studies and other subjects under poor bibliographic control or distribution.

After further design, however, the Conspectus was reshaped in two ways. First, the prescriptive implications of a "national policy" were greatly deemphasized in recognition of each library's local autonomy. Second, the potential scope of the Conspectus was broadened to include all fields of knowledge for the purpose of creating a national map of strong research collections that could point scholars to the best libraries for a particular field (Gwinn 1983).

As work on the RLG Conspectus proceeded, a number of issues dealing with its design and usefulness have emerged. One issue is whether a library's resources in a given field can be depicted clearly and meaningfully by a brief coded symbol based on the Conspectus's six-point rating scheme and four-point language spread. For example, a review of the Conspectuses of twenty collections in the French language discovered that the five libraries which awarded themselves a "4" (very high) rating owned anywhere from 31% to 62%–a very broad range–of the titles in the bibliographies used in their collection measures (Larson 1984).

Another issue is whether the six-point rating scale is useful in pointing scholars to the best collections, which are generally known anyway. Far more specific assistance is available either through access to the online catalogs of libraries that a scholar expects to visit, or through a search of the OCLC online union catalog, which contains the shared cataloging of about 4,500 libraries in twenty-six countries.

A third issue with the RLG Conspectus involves the weighing of costs and benefits of the Conspectus work itself with regard to subject bibliographers and library staff. While Conspectus experience will surely expand a librarian's knowledge about collection development, the substantial time required to evaluate the literature in even a single subject range could crowd out other professional responsibilities and interests. Some analysts have concluded that the shelflist project is superior to the Conspectus approach because it provides unequivocal linear measurements, as opposed to Conspectus ratings derived in unspecified ways, and because a shelflist count can be done by student assistants in much less time (Henige 1987).

OCLC/Amigos Collection Analysis Compact Disc

In a general critique of collection management technology, Osburn (1990) addressed the need for a new system that would combine the positive characteristics of the quantitative shelflist count and the qualitative Conspectus approach. About the same time, OCLC and AMIGOS introduced their collection analysis product, called Collection Analysis Compact Disc or CACD, a sophisticated system that offers an expedient means of evaluating a library's monograph holdings for a given subject in comparison to the aggregate holdings of a variety of peer groups.

Other papers provide detailed in-house reports of the CACD (Harrell forthcoming; Wilson).[1] Nevertheless, brief mention should be made of its pioneering capability to provide a bibliographic list of titles identified in gap or overlap analysis. Such lists can be limited, or sorted, by publication year(s), language, and peer-group holding distribution. For example, a printout of all French-language titles on international relations published since 1985, and held in at least 80% of ARL libraries (but not in one's own institution), can be done in a matter of minutes to identify potential acquisitions.

The CACD does not include non-book format materials or federal or state documents. Public university press titles, being considered strictly as "state documents," are not represented. Also, the disc incorporates just one cataloging record of a book, and so any title for which a library used a different record will erroneously be included in gap analysis.

Despite these imperfections, the CACD shows the best balance of quantitative measures, relative rankings, peer-group selection versatility, and sheer expediency. Collection management technology is no longer as hazy as before. Yet, the potential of the CACD to rationalize cooperative collection development across institutions is somewhat speculative. OCLC finds it technically feasible, though not yet cost-effective, to produce a disc in which each member of a consortium could be represented as a peer group of one, with the consortium constituting an additional collective peer group. In that framework, a library could compare itself one-on-one to any other member or to the consortium as a whole. Conceivably, such an approach would resolve the lack of highly detailed data on comparative collection management and provide a basis for improving the mix of cooperative arrangements.[2]

DISCUSSION

Underlying any general assessment of cooperative collection development is a dilemma of change in the American library system. On the one hand, generations of library leaders have long recognized the potentialities of resource sharing. Nearly forty years ago, for example, Downs made a precursory case for the contemporary model of "Combined Self-Interest":

From a practical point of view it is impossible for even the largest libraries, as they are now organized, to hold more than a fraction of the world's literature. Therefore, acquisition agreements among libraries would appear, theoretically at least, to be the logical and sensible solution. (1945, 411)

On the other hand, the principal characteristic of the American library system has been its extraordinary decentralization, each library having its own special mission and freedom of action.

Over the past decade, library leaders have proposed rather speculative and abstract strategies to resolve this dilemma. The model of "Combined Self-Interest" is essentially a "bubble up" strategy, whereby local consortia would evolve into regional and inter-regional arrangements: "Ultimately, cooperative collection development should provide a national network of dependencies and distributed responsibilities" (Mosher and Pankake 1983, 421).

An opposite approach is "top down." Battin, among others, has argued the need for a national cooperative strategy to overcome organizational difficulties of resource sharing at the local level:

> Many of our consortium and cooperative activities of the past have made the fundamental mistake of attempting to share resources without giving up our basic notion of the autonomous organization of libraries. . . . We must channel our energies into the design and development of effective cooperative activities at the national level, which will then enable us to discharge our obligations to our regional and local colleagues. (1980, 70)

The analysis of cooperative collection development presented here, focusing on certain generic properties of a loosely-coupled system, however, suggests some severe constraints on any grand cooperative scheme, whether "bubble up" or "top down" in design. One constraint is the essentially ambiguous relationship between means and ends in collection development, especially in academic institutions. Collection goals are idealistic. Selection of monographs is problematic, owing to wide variations in their number, cost, and subject classification from year to year. Collection management technology, even with the CACD, remains rather hazy.

Where means-ends relationships are so ambiguous, schemes of explicit goals cannot be representative of stable preference orders. Thus, academic institutions preserve their freedom of action within consortia, finding joint acquisition interests mostly on the margins of collection development areas. Indeed, such autonomy has been an explicit precondition of virtually all cooperative collection development models and programs.

What is known in any systematic way about other conditions of successful cooperative collection development programs can be readily summarized. First, cooperative collection development programs need easy and timely communications–a union catalog, similar methods of collection management, and a way to track titles and prices (Sartori 1989). Second, geographical proximity is highly advantageous. While a document delivery system works for photocopies, cooperative acquisition of monographs depends on two fundamentals. As White puts it, "one is a disaster, the other a myth":

> The disaster is the postal system; the myth is that interlibrary loan is a self-evident good that all libraries willingly share, because we all benefit from it. There has been an underlying assumption that everyone favors interlibrary loan because lending and borrowing cancel each other out, and therefore the economics do not have to be exact. We know, from our studies and others, that this is nonsense. There are borrowers and there are lenders, and to expect lending agencies to underwrite the poverty of borrowers is not only unfair, it is unconscionable as a management policy for librarians who should be allocating their scarce resources to serve their own clientele. . . . If regional resource sharing has any validity at all, then the cost of the system and the transactions should be recoverable from the savings at each local library. (1981, 38-39)

The optimal approach is a shuttle service for interlibrary loan between campuses within a radius of 100 miles or so. Greater distance may become a real handicap.

Third, members of a collection development consortium should have either complementary interests in certain specialized materials or dissimilar interests over a range of general materials. An example of the first sort involving academic libraries is the Triangle Research Libraries Group, in which Duke University is responsible for post-1917 Soviet periodicals and the University of North Carolina concentrates on pre-1917 titles (Dannelly 1985, 312). An example of the second sort–cooperation based on dissimilarity–is the arrangement between Washington State University and the University of Idaho, which are located eight miles apart. These schools have markedly different curricular and research interests, yet they consider their libraries to be a single extended (i.e., tightly-coupled) system (Roberts 1987).

The foregoing conditions generally fit a cluster of special libraries in an urban area with serial-based holdings in a relatively bounded subject, such as medicine or law. Titles and prices of serials are much easier to track than those of monographs. Cancellations of serials are far more visible and, without a ready alternative source, politically risky.

In conclusion, it may be useful to suggest future research needs in this area. A salient need is for the kind of study done by Hewitt and Shipman nearly ten years ago to assess how the collection development programs of academic libraries are faring. Such a survey, perhaps under the auspices of ARL, would provide information of much broader scope than the analysis presented here, which is based largely on social science models.

Another important need is for survey research on costs and benefits of cooperative collection development. Only one substantive study–on evaluation of membership in the Center for Research Libraries–has appeared (Rutledge and Swindler 1988). Several possible approaches exist: relative value (cost per transaction), absolute value (perceived value regardless of cost), and cost effectiveness (alternative sources for same material). Some writers, such as Dougherty, suggest that cooperative collection development should be measured on the basis of services rendered, not dollars saved (Dougherty 1988, 287). Others agree with White that economic accounting is necessary and appropriate.

NOTES

1. Editor's note: See also Joy, "The OCLC/AMIGOS Collection Analysis CD: A Unique Tool for Collection Evaluation and Development" in this volume.

2. For more information on the CACD contact the AMIGOS Bibliographic Council, Inc., 12200 Park Central Drive, Suite 500, Dallas, Texas 75251 (800)-843-8482 or Collette Mak, Marketing and User Services Division, OCLC, 6565 Frantz Road, Dublin, Ohio 43017-0702 (614)761-5053.

REFERENCES

Battin, Patricia. "Research Libraries in the Network Environment: The Case for Cooperation." *The Journal of Academic Librarianship* 6 (May 1980): 68-73.

Branin, Joseph J., David Farrell, and Mariann Tiblin. "The National Shelflist Count Project: Its History, Limitations, and Usefulness." *Library Resources & Technical Services* 25 (October/December 1985): 333-42.

Cohen, Michael D., James G. March, and Johan P. Olsen. "A Garbage Can Model of Organizational Choice." *Administrative Science Quarterly* 17 (March 1972): 1-25.

Cuadra, Carlos A., and Ruth J. Patrick. "Survey of Academic Library Consortia in the U.S." *College and Research Libraries* 33 (July 1972): 271-83.

Dannelly, Gay N. "Coordinating Cooperative Collection Development; A National Perspective: The LAPT Report." *Library Acquisitions: Practice and Theory* 9 (1985): 307-15.

Dougherty, Richard M. "A Conceptual Framework for Organized Resource Sharing and Shared Collection Development Programs." *The Journal of Academic Librarianship* 14 (November 1988): 287-91.

Downs, Robert B. "American Library Cooperation in Review." *College and Research Libraries* 6 (September 1945, part II): 407-15.

Gwinn, Nancy E., and Paul H. Mosher. "Coordinating Collection Development: The RLG Conspectus." *College and Research Libraries* 44 (March 1983): 128-40.

Harrell, Jeanne. "Use of the OCLC/AMIGOS Collection Analysis CD to Determine Comparative Collection Strength in English and American Literature: A Case Study." *Technical Services Quarterly*. Forthcoming.

Henige, David. "Epistemological Dead End and Ergonomic Disaster? The North American Collections Inventory Project." *The Journal of Academic Librarianship* 13 (September 1987): 209-13.

Hewitt, Joe A., and John S. Shipman. "Cooperative Collection Development Among Research Libraries in the Age of Networking: Report of a Survey of ARL Libraries." *Advances in Library Automation and Networking* 1 (1987): 189-232.

Jones, C. Lee. "A Cooperative Serial Acquisition Program: Thoughts on a Response to Mounting Fiscal Pressures." *Bulletin of the Medical Library Association* 62 (April 1974): 120.

Larson, Jeffry. "The RLG French Literature Collection Assessment Project." *Collection Management* 6 (Spring/Summer 1984): 97-114.

Lutz, Frank W. "Tightening Up Loose Coupling in Organizations of Higher Education." *Administrative Science Quarterly* 27 (December 1982): 653-69.

Mosher, Paul H., and Marcia Pankake. "A Guide to Coordinated and Cooperative Collection Development." *Library Resources and Technical Services* 27 (October/December 1983): 417-31.

Osburn, Charles B. "Collection Development and Management." In *Academic Libraries: Research Perspectives,* edited by Mary Jo Lynch and Arthur Young. Chicago: American Library Association, 1990.

Roberts, Elizabeth P. "Cooperation, Collection Management, and Scientific Journals." *College and Research Libraries* 48 (May 1987): 247-51.

Rutledge, John, and Luke Swindler. "Evaluating Membership in a Resource-Sharing Program: The Center for Research Libraries." *College and Research Libraries* 49 (September 1988): 409-24.

Sartori, Eva Martin. "Regional Collection Development of Serials." *Collection Management* 11 (1989): 69-76.

Schwartz, Charles A. "Book Selection, Collection Development, and Bounded Rationality." *College and Research Libraries* 50 (May 1989): 328-43.

Stuart-Stubbs, Basil. "An Historical Look at Resource Sharing." *Library Trends* 23 (April 1975): 649-64.

Weber, David. "A Century of Cooperative Programs among Research Libraries." *College and Research Libraries* 37 (May 1976): 205-21.

Weick, Karl E. "Educational Institutions as Loosely-Coupled Systems." *Administrative Science Quarterly* 21 (March 1976): 1-19.

White, Herbert S. "Publishers, Libraries, and Costs of Journal Subscriptions in Times of Funding Retrenchment." *The Library Quarterly* 46 (October 1976): 359-71.

White, Herbert S. "Factors in the Decision By Individuals and Libraries to Place or Cancel Subscriptions to Scholarly and Research Journals." *The Library Quarterly* 50 (July 1980): 287-309.

White, Herbert S. "Strategies and Alternatives in Dealing with the Serials Management Budget." In *Serials Collection Development: Choices and Strategies,* edited by Sul H. Lee. Ann Arbor, Mich.: Pierian Press, 1981.

Wilson, Flo. "Comparative Collection Analysis: Using the AMIGOS/OCLC Collection Analysis CD." Unpublished manuscript.

Building a Nationwide Bibliographic Database: The Role of Local Shared Automated Systems

Louella V. Wetherbee

SUMMARY. The creation of a nationwide bibliographic database (NBD) has been the shared responsibility of the national libraries, the major bibliographic utilities, and individual libraries. Libraries have contributed their local cataloging records to the national hosts, the bibliographic utilities, which in turn, made these records widely available. The emergence of local shared automated library systems has introduced a new set of stakeholders into this environment. Their participation in bibliographic networking will result in a decentralized nationwide bibliographic database stored in multiple locations.

Library automation, in general, and local shared systems, in particular, have increased the scope and complexity of library cooperative efforts. This paper addresses the actual and potential impact of local shared automated library systems on the development of a comprehensive nationwide bibliographic database (NBD).

Louella V. Wetherbee is a Library and Network Management Consultant based in Dallas, TX. She holds BA and MLS degrees from the University of Texas at Austin.

This paper is based on a research project undertaken for the Library of Congress Network Advisory Committee in 1990-91. The project was funded by the Council on Library Resources. The complete report of the project was originally published as part of a *NAC Planning Paper*. The author would like to acknowledge the contributions of members of NAC in the preparation of this paper.

© 1992 by The Haworth Press, Inc. All rights reserved.

Over the past 20 years, the Library of Congress Network Advisory Committee (NAC) has monitored, studied, and described the major changes and significant trends in the development of nationwide library and information networking. NAC has investigated the role of many groups and organizations in the library and information networking arena including the role of local shared automated library systems.

NAC members, who represent diverse segments of the networking community, evolved a common vision of library networking. This vision is based, in part, on an

> . . . environment in which libraries can provide each individual in the United States with equal opportunity of access to resources that will satisfy their and society's information needs and interests . . . . (Library of Congress Network Advisory Committee 1987, 5)

The development of this environment is understood to include a widely accessible national bibliographic database. NAC commissioned a study in 1990 of local shared automated systems in an effort to identify and describe broad trends at the local level that may determine the future size, scope, location, and completeness of the NBD. The study focused on twenty-nine local shared automated systems.

Local shared systems are an important part of the national bibliographic and information network. To date, they have not been systematically inventoried, nor described. While this paper does not constitute a full inventory of the local shared automated systems environment, it does identify and describe trends evident from a review of a representative group of local shared system organizations in terms of their database resources and their links to national database providers and to each other.

There were three reasons for the decision to focus on local systems sharing a single computer or computer configuration. First, it provided manageability in terms of numbers while still assuring diversity. Second it multiplied the number of libraries whose interface with the NBD could be investigated, at least on the level of contribution of bibliographic records and database developments.

Third, and most important, the advent of large shared databases outside the major utilities represents a significant new force in the evolving nationwide database and is, in itself, one of the major points of impact on the national library and information services environment.

The number of local shared automated systems in operation is not known, and no current adequate directories exist. Several lists and specialized directories were consulted. These included (1) the chapter on networks and consortia from the *ALA Directory* (Networks . . . 1989), (2) a list of thirty-four network profiles prepared by Elaine Hartman Lemmond (1990), and (3) a directory prepared by the LITA Consortia/Automated Systems Interest Group which lists ninety-seven systems (Burke and Bragg 1991). The 1989 ASCLA (Association of Specialized Cooperative Library Agencies) Report on Library Cooperation was also consulted (Wilkins 1990).

The primary source of information about the local systems was a series of extensive telephone and personal interviews which the author conducted with senior staff of the local shared systems between July 1990 and March 1991. The bibliographic utilities provided recent information about their programs and plans. The information reported in this paper reflects the environment at that time.

DEFINING THE NATIONWIDE
BIBLIOGRAPHIC DATABASE

Until recently there has been a common assumption in the library community that authoritative information about the combined bibliographic resources of the nation would reside principally at the national level, stored and maintained by the bibliographic utilities and the national libraries. It is increasingly clear, however, that a distributed nationwide bibliographic database is rapidly evolving from hundreds, and eventually thousands, of local databases. This shift toward greater emphasis on the local resource database has long term implications for the development of a comprehensive nationwide database of bibliographic records and holdings.

A major effect of the development of local shared automated

systems is the decentralization of the national database. The nodes of the decentralized database will not be effectively interconnected for some time to come, resulting in an increasingly heterogeneous set of bibliographic databases residing at local, state, and national levels. Standards will bend to local needs, redundancy will be the rule, and overlapping coverage will be commonplace.

As a result of these trends, there will be no single national level "database of record." The Library of Congress (LC) will continue to be the major provider of quality bibliographic information, in tandem with the major research libraries and bibliographic utilities. Neither LC, nor any other national level organization, however, will be able to control the contents and scope of the NBD. The NBD will be composed of an interconnected web of local databases. The creators and builders of these local databases will have to make decisions about database standards and content without full consideration of the implications for national resource sharing.

In 1978 NAC developed a series of definitions for the various components of a national database. The following two definitions are taken from that glossary:

> "National Library Network Database": A compatible set of machine-readable files of bibliographic data constructed according to network standards and designed to support national library network services . . . also called the network database.
> "National Library Network Union Catalog": . . . a union catalog or set of union catalogs (separate union catalogs may be necessary for specific library groups) derived from the national library network database. Entry points will be standardized by centers of responsibility and record redundancy will be minimized . . . . (Buchinski 1978, 7-8)

The components of this structure as foreseen in the 1978 NAC paper included a centralized network coordinating agency, a number of bibliographic utilities, and a series of regional service centers, all working together to serve the clientele of the nation's libraries. The emergence of local shared automated systems as a key component of the developing network structure was not forecast, although it was assumed that groupings of libraries (e.g., medical, law, etc.) might want special network services.

The network coordinating agency was supposed to "design the technical network configuration, determine legal and organizational structure, and specify the configuration of the national database(s)" as well as "maintain network files, monitor authentication and validation of contributed records, provide access to network files, and, in cooperation with the U.S. library community, maintain the codes and standards of the network" (Buchinski 1978, 18-19). In practice, the existing bibliographic utilities, plus the national libraries and bibliographic programs, perform most of these functions. The Library of Congress sets bibliographic standards and the utilities impose these standards on their users to some extent. National projects such as CONSER perform authentication of subsets of the national database.

The "National Library Network Database" will probably be quite different from NAC's original concept. The term "Nationwide Bibliographic Database" may be a better way to describe the current data sets that compose the network database. Early network plans included provision for verification of locally produced records which, once authenticated, would become the national record. It is now clear that the NBD will be decentralized and redundant and that authentication will not be widespread.

BUILDING THE NATIONWIDE
BIBLIOGRAPHIC DATABASE

The rise of local automated systems over the past ten years has created an environment in which the creation of the NBD is shared among large numbers of libraries through the creation of large files of converted catalog records. At the same time that local libraries were developing shared automated systems, the telecommunications links between and among libraries began to change. Some large libraries began to take advantage of in-place telecommunications networks (e.g., the Internet) to share information. The first group of libraries to recognize the potential implications of Internet connections were academic libraries, where the telecommunications network links already existed within and among many institutions of higher education. It is probable that, as the National Research and Education Network (NREN)[1] develops, these libraries will begin to shift their bibliographic and resource sharing activities away from dedicated networks to more broadly based multi-purpose networks.

The library community has focused considerable attention on converting library catalogs of print materials into standardized machine readable records. Many local online catalogs have been built on the basis of this catalog conversion. The development of these stand alone and shared local online catalogs (OPACs) parallels the emergence of the Internet as a conduit for the transmission of a broad array of information resources. Only some of these resources are bibliographic in nature; most are not under standard bibliographic control, as it is understood in the library community. Some libraries and networks have begun to make their OPACs accessible over the Internet. The bibliographic utilities are also beginning to offer access to selected databases over the Internet.

The library community has begun to expand the types of material in local library OPACs to include tables of contents, indexes, journal abstracts, and enhanced MARC records. Most local shared automated systems have not yet begun to address the demand for access to external and/or non-bibliographic databases. But a few of the systems investigated in this study have already begun to expand their systems to include these files.

At the regional and local level, discussions between the library community and the network planners are also starting. It is essential that all segments of the library community be brought into the dialogue about networked information resources. The knowledge-base has not yet developed among smaller and medium sized libraries, especially those outside the academic environment, that will enable local libraries to connect to the Internet. Smaller shared systems and individual libraries will be hard pressed to find the money to connect to the Internet without external funding until connectivity is understood as a central library service.

Many libraries and library systems currently have no access to the Internet and the broader array of information resources that such access implies. For a great many smaller libraries, resource sharing is limited to local networks connecting a few libraries. Some of these libraries may, in turn, have access to one or more of the bibliographic utilities. There is relatively little direct sharing of records or holdings of libraries between and among local shared systems; resource sharing still depends on access to one of the national bibliographic utilities.

THE RISE OF SHARED LOCAL AUTOMATED SYSTEMS

The term "local shared automated system," as used in this paper, means an automated library system being shared by two or more libraries within a state or interstate. The study targeted systems with a significant portion of their records already in machine-readable form in a shared database and accessible to system users through an online catalog. The systems studied are geographically diverse and included state-wide networks, multi-type networks, single-type networks, and single library systems with multiple sites.

The twenty-nine systems in the study group are varied in terms of organization and purpose. Twenty-two systems are multi-type, one is public only and six are academic only. Several of the multi-type networks are composed mostly of public libraries, although they are nominally multi-type. The systems are located in fifteen different states and most operate within one state. It is difficult to ascertain with any certainty the actual number of libraries directly served, but it is above 1000. At least fifteen of the twenty-nine are either independent 501(C)3 non-profits or programs of larger non-profits.

There is wide diversity in terms of local automated system vendors among the twenty-nine organizations. Six sites use the NOTIS system; four each use Geac and CLSI; two each use DRA, UTLAS, and LS2000; one each uses INLEX, CARL, Dynix, and Carlyle. The remainder are locally developed systems.

The local systems databases vary from less than 100,000 bibliographic records to over six million records. At least six of the systems do not maintain a USMARC record database. For those that do not, however, most are upgrading their records to the USMARC standard. The acceptance of USMARC as the desirable standard is universal among this group of systems.

The data available to build statistical profiles of the systems are inadequate. The number of bibliographic records in the local system database does not always coincide with the number of unique titles. Some systems do not know the number of unique titles in the database. It would be useful to have a universally accepted way to count bibliographic records and holdings statements. Currently the ability to give a count of holdings depends solely on the capabilities of the local system vendor software. Even unique title counts are questionable since it is not clear that records which are no longer held by a library are systematically deleted from the shared database.

Most of the systems investigated have achieved a high level of conversion of member catalog records. The lowest estimate of converted records loaded into the local system was 60%. Five systems report their member libraries are 100% converted. Seven are at least 90% converted and another seven are at least 70% converted. It is likely that increasing numbers of system libraries will begin to seek external source files for inclusion in the local database since catalog conversion is nearing an end.

FOUR LOCAL SHARED AUTOMATED SYSTEM MODELS

While there is no single model of local shared system development, these four system models are indicative of emerging trends. The models include an independent multi-type system with strong public participation, an independent academic research library network, a state sponsored academic network, and a state agency based state-wide academic library network. With minor variations, all twenty-nine systems fall into one of these four categories.[2] For each model, these attributes are described: the system database, its relationship to the national database, system participant cataloging sources, and system linking plans.

CircCess:
An Evolving Multi-Type System

CircCess is a program of the Capitol Region Library Council in Windsor, Connecticut. It is a multi-type cooperative of thirty-two members including nine academic and twenty-three public libraries in the Hartford area. All ongoing costs are paid by member fees. Each member pays a flat annual fee and the balance of the costs are allocated based on the number of system terminals and circulation transactions.

The network serves as " . . . a means of providing access to the books and materials in all member libraries by means of an automated circulation system" (CircCess 1989). Recently, the goals of the system seem to be expanding beyond circulation. This is a common trend among other multi-type local automated systems which are upgrading mature circulation systems and creating OPACs.

The CircCess database contains 1.2 million bibliographic records to which over three million copy statements are attached. The database is accessible on 208 terminals at fifty sites. The current Geac 9000 system does not handle the USMARC format, but the database is being systematically upgraded to full MARC records in anticipation of the installation of a new automated system. Multiple sources have been used to create the new database, including AMIGOS, SOLINET, OCLC, and the Library Corporation. Only OCLC is used for current cataloging. Although exact figures are not known, at least 80% of the cataloged materials of the libraries in CircCess have been added to the database. The new database will be much more than a compendium of brief records for circulation transactions, the purpose of the original database. Plans for database enhancements in the new system include mounting local databases. The ability to load and access external databases is a selection criterion for a new system.

CircCess operates as an OCLC cluster, a common practice among multi-type systems of this nature. Nineteen network members are full OCLC users. Cluster libraries input brief records into GEAC which are printed daily and searched in OCLC. A CircCess cataloger then adds a single three character cluster symbol to OCLC to satisfy OCLC contract requirements. Weekly OCLC multi-institutional tapes are loaded into Geac.

Cataloging must be full USMARC cataloging based on AACR2. CircCess has written input standards to guide local catalogers. While the network does not expect any change in cataloging sources, less costly alternatives would be considered if available.

CircCess connects to the nationwide bibliographic database through OCLC. Since September 1989, member libraries have contributed 100% of member cataloging to OCLC. No records are contributed to other utilities, but about 80% of CircCess OCLC titles are loaded into the state CD-ROM public access catalog.

The actual percentage of the total CircCess database which is represented in OCLC is not known. There are no current plans or funds for further contribution of local retrospective files. CircCess is not currently linked to any other local automated system nor does the system have access to the Internet. Although CircCess loads all new records into OCLC, CircCess is not an OCLC ILL provider. Therefore, the presence of the CircCess cluster symbol on OCLC is not very meaningful, since it is not possible for a potential borrowing library to connect the title with a specific library in Connecticut.

CircCess is typical of older multi-type circulation systems that are upgrading the quality of their bibliographic databases and enlarging their scope of service. These local shared systems are moving beyond circulation functions as they begin to create OPACs and investigate the addition of local and/or external databases to their system, perhaps as value-added services.

Like many other local area multi-type networks, CircCess is almost entirely funded by the local participants. Contribution of records and participation in national level networking is going to be dependent on external funding unless the local benefit is perceived as fairly immediate and direct.

TRLN:
AN INDEPENDENT ACADEMIC LIBRARY NETWORK

TRLN, the Triangle Research Libraries Network, is composed of eight academic libraries in the Research Triangle of North Carolina. The participating libraries at Duke University, the University of North Carolina, and North Carolina State University, already had a history of cooperation in collection development before they embarked on a shared automation program. The original purpose of TRLN was to create an online catalog to be shared by all the libraries.

The network is governed by a ten member board including the library directors and the provosts of the three universities. For the past five years, about one-half of the annual budget has come from private foundation funds. This is an unusual characteristic for a network when compared to the others studied. Network operating funds are rarely provided by grants, although start-up and capital equipment funds are often sought from foundations.

TRLN operates locally developed database software called BIS (Bibliographic Information System) supporting 230 terminals. The OPAC and circulation functions are fully operational. Other functions as well as external database searching capability will be added only as part of future system upgrades using vendor developed software.

The database contains 2,527,707 bibliographic records. No holdings statistics are available. The database is composed of three separate databases, but a single search results in a merged record display if desired. All USMARC formats are supported except MRDF (Machine-Readable Data Files), but the system cannot output a MARC record.

All current cataloging is from OCLC. Each institution does its own cataloging locally and tapeloads records into BIS. No changes are currently foreseen in cataloging sources. TRLN contributes all current cataloging to OCLC and 99% of BIS database records are in OCLC. TRLN members have a commitment to tapeload into the utility any additional retrospective conversion records that are done.

TRLN is connected to LincNet, a telecommunications network for the sixteen institutions of the University of North Carolina system. Each LincNet site can search BIS for ILL and resource sharing purposes, but not for bibliographic control purposes. Access includes both dial-in and direct connection via campus networks. The access is currently available only to library staff, but faculty members at TRLN institutions will be able to search across the network.

TRLN has the potential to be a cataloging resource database, given its rich database and its links to other libraries. In the near term, because of its current software configuration and local goals, it is not likely that TRLN will provide direct cataloging services to other libraries. Since each TRLN library partner has a commitment to strong individual OCLC participation, the emerging practice of posting holdings for second and subsequent titles against the first downloaded occurrence of an OCLC record in the local system database is not likely to be implemented by TRLN. All the libraries will continue to catalog on OCLC first, then load records into the local database.

Florida Center for Library Automation: A State-Wide Academic Library Network

The Florida Center for Library Automation (FCLA) is a large academic library network that has developed rapidly since 1984. FCLA is a state agency under the state university system. It is administratively attached to the University of Florida. The Center supports nine university libraries with thirteen autonomous library components in fifty sites. The state mandate for FCLA is reflected in the enabling legislative appropriation which states that

> . . . all university libraries will be supported by single soft-ware systems for principal library functions, that files will be available . . . for other educational units of the state, and that required computer systems will be located and operated by the State University System Regional Data Centers . . . .(Dalehite 1989, 208-209)

FCLA maintains a single NOTIS system installation supporting separate databases for each institution. FCLA supports cataloging, acquisitions, authorities, an OPAC, circulation, and serials. Each institution maintains separate bibliographic files. Autonomous libraries within an institution may choose to maintain separate bibliographic records. There are 6.3 million bibliographic records, but the number of unique titles is not known. All records are in the USMARC format, and the system supports all the USMARC formats.

Ninety to one hundred percent of the total cataloged holdings of FCLA participants are represented in the FCLA database. LC subject authority records have been loaded. The original database was created from a combination of OCLC, ReMarc, and BROD-ART records. Like TRLN, FCLA plans to load external databases using appropriate vendor developed software.

Ninety-seven percent of current cataloging loaded into FCLA is from OCLC. The remaining three percent comes from RLIN. The RLIN records, however, are re-keyed into OCLC, since FCLA cannot accept RLIN tapes. OCLC records are downloaded to NOTIS using a custom PC interface. The interface can also accept diskette record files from vendor approval plans.

In terms of FCLA holdings represented at the national level, OCLC is the major repository. On both a retrospective and current basis, the coverage is almost complete. All university libraries in FCLA comply with the state library requirement to post holdings in OCLC. Probably less than 3% of the total FCLA database are not in OCLC; these items are old ReMarc records. In addition, the University of Florida and Florida State have about two million records in RLIN representing cataloging up to 1988.

Since the FCLA members continue to catalog on OCLC, the currency of their records on the national system is maintained. The bibliographic maintenance function will erode over time, however, as more and more FCLA libraries view the local database as the database of record.

The FCLA OPAC is on the Internet and is also accessible via dial-in. While FCLA has no links to other local systems at this time, the system is mandated to link to other state systems and make their records widely available. The most likely first link will be to the emerging state community college system which has chosen Data Research Associates (DRA) as its vendor.

Given the size of its database and the state directive to make its files available to other educational units, it seems inevitable that FCLA will begin to look more and more like a utility. Only ten of the twenty-nine community colleges in the new system are OCLC members. As they seek conversion sources, it would be reasonable for them to consider FCLA as one option.

The clear purpose of FCLA provided by its state legislative mandate and the unity provided by the purely academic focus of its members is a factor which gives it great strength as an organization. FCLA is a probable model for a strong regional bibliographic resource provider, still linked to the national database, but gradually moving toward more and more bibliographic autonomy. Given the strong OCLC connection for most FCLA libraries, reinforced by state library requirements to post holdings nationally, no major changes are likely in the next three years. The choice of NOTIS as the network automated system positions the network to tap into other developing NOTIS databases outside the region if it is politically and bibliographically appropriate to do so.

NHAIS:
A State-Wide System for New Hampshire

NHAIS is another example of state driven networking. The network was created in 1983 by an act of the state legislature and is composed of over 260 libraries of all types. Funding has been predominantly state and federal in the start-up phase, but there is a definite trend toward local funding for ongoing support of network activities. NHAIS operates a four node system based on Ameritech's LS2000 hardware and software. Each node is connected to the others via microwave and land links and each node can search every other node with a single log-on function. Over 500 terminals are supported, although not all the terminals are capable of multi-node log-on and searching. Approximately 75% of the state's population has access to an NHAIS node and hence to the resources in any of the other nodes.

The system maintains a dozen dial access and several 800 inbound WATS lines for local library access to the nodes. ILL is available intra-node on three nodes and the state plans to support more inter-node access. NHAIS is working with the state college and university council on a project to tie the systems together using telecommunications links provided by NEARnet.

The four connected databases contain a total of 1,266,912 records spread across four nodes. The number of unique titles is not known. Ninety-nine percent of the database is composed of full USMARC records. All USMARC formats are supported. All current cataloging records for participating libraries are added, and 90% of post-1980 cataloging records have been loaded; conversion of pre-1980 records by various methods is ongoing. In addition to the USMARC catalog database, NHAIS maintains MARC-like files indexing state newspapers and also has a status-of-bills legislative database.

Ninety-five percent of current cataloging added to the system is OCLC cataloging. A small number of libraries receive USMARC records on tape from book vendors. These records are input directly into the local node, but are not contributed to OCLC. NHAIS does not anticipate changing cataloging sources in the near future, although the nodes could begin to search each other and claim records if they do not require cataloging cards. NHAIS is a U.S. Newspaper Program (USNP) participant. The database contains the USNP records and exploded holdings so that system users can identify the actual library holding the desired piece. This type of tiered representation of records with a summary statement at the national level and comprehensive holdings at the local level is one model for future national/local database interfacing.

NHAIS is an OCLC network. No records from NHAIS are contributed to any other utility. Approximately 90% of all local cataloging is in OCLC, although many holdings appear as processing center codes. The state library has always handled cataloging for the public libraries in the state, but access is provided because the local nodes can identify the holding libraries for resource sharing purposes. This method, while different from networks in states that require direct OCLC contribution of records, has the same practical result.

NHAIS has plans to add a state-wide union list of serials to the database. They are also working on a non-MARC based resource directory of public and private agencies with a focus on natural resources. Commercially available databases will also be integrated into the system menu of options.

COMPARISON OF THE FOUR MODELS

In some respects the NHAIS system shares several characteristics with the FCLA system. There is strong state support, even a state mandate, to provide services to a defined set of libraries. This clarity of purpose and stability provided by the state umbrella is an indicator of long term network viability. In comparison, private not-for-profit shared systems such as CircCess must be aggressively entrepreneurial in order to attract and maintain a stable membership base over time. Like FCLA, NHAIS has the technical capability to function as a state cataloging utility for libraries within its sphere of interest. A strong commitment to OCLC has slowed this move.

Local system practice varies widely among the systems studied in terms of acceptable sources of cataloging copy. For example, three of the shared systems in the study group, Bibliomation, ILLI-NET Online and MSUS/PALS, require that all incoming current database records be OCLC records. In those cases, libraries who individually chose another cataloging source for any reason would not be able to meet membership requirements or would have to negotiate an exception. While local systems certainly do not control local cataloging decisions, they are in a strong position to influence both the source and standards for local library cataloging in much the way that the bibliographic utilities influenced local cataloging practices in the 1970's and 1980's.

LOCAL SHARED SYSTEMS AND THE NBD: CURRENT STATUS AND TRENDS

The current interface between local shared automated library systems and the NBD is the extent to which local records are represented in the national resource databases held by the utilities. WLN, UTLAS, and RLIN each store significant portions of the NBD, but are less complete than OCLC.

Regardless of the utility used, the emphasis on the creation and maintenance of local system databases will increase. Local system participants will gradually shift their focus away from contributing to and maintaining records in the national utility databases. The "database of record" for most local systems in the future is not going to be the utility database, but the local system database. Gerald Lowell (1990) described this trend in a survey of twenty-five ARL (Association for Research Libraries) institutions. He noted that both cataloging and bibliographic maintenance will be supported increasingly and mainly on the local system.

While the same trend which Lowell noted of movement toward local bibliographic maintenance is anecdotally evident in the profiled systems, the shift to local database emphasis will be gradual. It will depend on several factors: (1) the ability of local systems to fully support cataloging and catalog maintenance; (2) the resolution of issues concerning contribution of current cataloging once maintenance moves off the utility; (3) the definition of bibliographic standards at the local system level acceptable to a generation of utility-trained catalogers; and (4) the determination of rights of local systems to reuse, sell, or otherwise distribute OCLC-derived records. The clean-up and upgrade of databases will increase the difficulty in identifying the original sources of cataloging records. Is an OCLC record still an OCLC record, after being authorized by Utlas, merged by SOLINET, and enhanced with a contents note from a commercial supplier that also links the record to the full text of the item?

CONCLUSION

The commitment of libraries participating in local shared systems to contribute their records to the NBD through uploading to the utilities seems to remain high. Of the twenty-nine systems in the study, only one does not contribute records to a utility. A key reason for contributing records is that many library systems continue to be dependent upon utilities for cataloging. As long as they are, they will probably continue to honor their contractual obligations to contribute their current cataloging to the utilities. Most local shared systems have a strong interest in the concept of a national database, but that concern is secondary to the development of the local system database. Local systems will continue to post holdings to the NBD if they can do it as an integral part of local catalog maintenance and if it is cost effective. In some cases state agency obligations are an additional incentive to post holdings, particularly to OCLC.

Many local automated library systems already have the ability to support cataloging and maintenance. There will be a slow trend in the direction of using local online cataloging software and local database records for shared cataloging. This will result in the erosion of cataloging activity and revenue for the utilities.

In the future, the local shared automated systems will interconnect to share and exchange data. Local systems will seek ways to lower cataloging costs further by creating reciprocal cataloging agreements similar to current ILL agreements. This change will be gradual and will affect smaller libraries more. Large research and academic libraries will continue to depend on the utilities for most of their cataloging needs for the foreseeable future.

Local system libraries will demand more efficient uploading and downloading to and from the utilities. Tapeloading will gradually decrease to be replaced by electronic transfer of records and holdings.

As local systems complete conversion of book and journal collections, they will start to add external files, often purchased from the commercial sector. They will also actively seek ways to add value to their databases by mounting locally produced non-bibliographic files. As they add such files, they will actively seek ways to charge external users for access to offset ongoing maintenance costs and provide an income stream.

The decentralization of cataloging which will result from the move of catalog maintenance to the local system database (already underway in large research libraries) has the potential to degrade the standards for cataloging quality that have evolved since the inception of large scale participation in the utilities. Such a degradation might be prejudicial to the quality of information in both national and local databases. A few of the larger local systems, particularly those based on research libraries, may begin to function like bibliographic utilities, but this change will be gradual.

Local automated library systems will explore interconnection through the Internet. Integration of non-academic local shared systems will be very slow in most cases. There is a major educational task ahead to inform local shared automated systems of the practical steps they can take to gain access to the Internet and to define appropriate levels of participation for the various types of shared systems.

There is going to be gradual erosion of the completeness and currency of records and holdings at the national level. The Nationwide Bibliographic Database will evolve into multiple levels. The national level, best represented by OCLC, will contain bibliographic records, summary holdings data, preservation information, and other content files such as indexes and abstracts. At the local level, there will be a proliferation of overlapping local databases which may duplicate much of the information held at the national level, as well as retain more complete holdings and location data and unique local files. "Local" in these cases may be defined as municipal, county-wide, regional, campus-level, or larger constituencies. Hierarchies will be less important since networks can horizontally connect quite easily without the need for extensive administrative structure.

The focus of database development and resource sharing has shifted from a few very large organizations to hundreds of local systems and local library databases. New organizations have formed to create, maintain, and manage these databases at the local level. These organizations are under-represented as a collective force in policy making. Yet it is among these organizations–and particularly those which are centered around major research libraries–that the models for future resource sharing and database developments will evolve.

NOTES

1. Editor's note: See Summerhill, "Internetworking: New Opportunities and Challenges in Resource Sharing" in this volume.
2. Statistical profiles and brief narrative descriptions of all twenty-nine systems are available from the Network Development Office at the Library of Congress.

REFERENCES

Buchinski, Edwin J. *Initial Considerations for a Nationwide Database.* Network Planning Paper, no. 3. Washington, D.C.: Library of Congress Network Development Office, 1978.
Burke, Marianne, and Peter Bragg. *Directory of Library Consortia with Cooperative Automated Systems.* Chicago: Library and Information Technology Association, 1991.

[CircCess flyer]. Windsor, CT: Capitol Region Library Council, 27 March 1989.

Dalehite, Michele. "Florida Center for Library Automation: The Organization." *Advances in Library Automation and Networking* 3 (1989): 205-224.

Lemmond, Elaine Hartman. "Network Profiles." VTLS, Inc., November 15, 1990.

Library of Congress Network Advisory Committee. *Library Networking: Statement of a Common Vision.* Network Planning Paper, no. 15. Washington, D.C.: Library of Congress Network Development Office, 1987.

Lowell, Gerald. "Local Systems and Bibliographic Utilities in 1992: A Large Research Library Perspective." *Journal of Academic Librarianship* 16 (July 1990): 140-144.

"Networks, Consortia and Other Cooperative Library Organizations." In *American Library Directory, 1989-90,* edited by Beverley McDonough and Edgar Adcock, Jr., 2155-2176. New York: R.R. Bowker, 1989.

Wilkins, Jean E. *The Report on Library Cooperation 1989.* Chicago: Association of Specialized and Cooperative Library Agencies, 1990.

Resource Sharing
and System Interconnection

Bernard G. Sloan

SUMMARY. This article briefly describes ILLINET Online, a resource sharing network for the state of Illinois. The constituency of the network, recent usage statistics, and the development of recent technological changes are discussed. Future plans are also outlined.

BACKGROUND

ILLINET Online is a union catalog and automated resource sharing network in Illinois. The system has been in operation as a resource sharing network since July 1980. ILLINET Online serves a dual purpose: to support local operations for forty Illinois libraries and to provide a statewide union catalog and interlibrary loan network. The system serves as both a local catalog and a circulation system for each of the state-supported universities, twenty-one private colleges and universities, four community colleges, a state-supported high school for gifted students in mathematics and the sciences, and the Illinois State Library, the state's library agency as well as library to state government.

ILLINET Online also serves as a union catalog and interlibrary loan network for the 2,600 libraries in Illinois that belong to the Illinois Library and Information Network (ILLINET). More than 800 libraries in Illinois participate in the ILLINET/OCLC program. The OCLC cataloging activity of these 800 libraries is used as a source of data entry for ILLINET Online. The catalog presently

Bernard G. Sloan is Director of the Illinois Library Computer Systems Office.

© 1992 by The Haworth Press, Inc. All rights reserved.

holds records representing 7.5 million titles and 20 million volumes. Users can make use of a number of search qualifiers, or "scopes," to search the entire database or subsets, such as individual libraries or geographic regions. Each of the 2,600 ILLINET libraries has a patron record in the circulation system which they can use to directly request materials on behalf of their patrons, via extensive dial access facilities. Document delivery is handled via the Intersystems Library Delivery Service (ILDS).

RESOURCE SHARING THROUGH
ILLINET ONLINE

ILLINET Online has supported resource sharing activities for more than a decade. Resource sharing activity was at record levels during fiscal year 1991. System users logged 591,142 interlibrary loan transactions during the year (July 1990 through June 1991), an increase of nearly 11% over fiscal year 1990. ILLINET Online resource sharing activity is divided into three categories, based on the source of the borrowing transaction: the Illinois Library Computer Systems Organization direct participant libraries, the regional multi-type library systems, and the state's local libraries. The forty Illinois Library Computer Systems Organization (ILCSO) direct participant libraries (i.e., those libraries that use the system for both local and interlibrary operations) initiated 448,045 interlibrary loan transactions against the holdings of other direct participants, an increase of 6.35% over FY 1990.

The transactions initiated against the holdings of the forty direct participants by the interlibrary loan departments of the eighteen regional multi-type library systems in Illinois are initiated on behalf of a library system's member libraries, who have initiated the transaction at the request of a local patron. These eighteen library systems initiated a total of 99,905 interlibrary loan transactions against the holdings of the forty direct participants, a drop of 9.5% from fiscal year 1990. Some decrease had been expected, as several hundred system member libraries had started borrowing materials directly from the libraries during fiscal year 1991, rather than going through the systems' interlibrary loan offices.

More than 400 of the state's local libraries of all types initiated 43,192 interlibrary loan transactions against the holdings of the direct participants in this first full fiscal year of expanded dial access capabilities. Public libraries led the way, with 60.8% of the requests, followed by academic libraries (not including the direct participants) with 19.6%, school libraries with 12.1%, and special libraries with 7.5%.

Perhaps the most interesting aspect of the FY 1991 statistics is that the expanded dial access interlibrary loan activity did not have a significant impact on borrowing by the eighteen library systems. Some people had anticipated that the first full year of dial access interlibrary loan activity would displace borrowing by the library system ILL departments. While there was some displacement, activity by the eighteen library systems dropped by only 9,518 transactions from the FY 1990 level, while the state's local libraries directly initiated more than 43,000 interlibrary loan transactions.

Recent dial access usage statistics demonstrate that libraries of all types continue to make use of ILLINET Online as a resource sharing tool. The state's libraries initiated 3,860 interlibrary loan requests via dial access during November 1991, an increase of nearly 20% over the 3,227 dial access ILL requests placed during November 1990. Dial access libraries initiated 25,790 online catalog searches during November 1991. As a matter of comparison, the dial access libraries as a group made more extensive use of the catalog than did the patrons and staff of twenty-eight direct participant libraries individually. In addition, the busiest dial access library regularly initiates more interlibrary loan transactions on ILLINET Online than a dozen direct participants do individually.

DIVERSE RESOURCES AND SYSTEMS

The tremendous success of ILLINET Online as a resource sharing tool demonstrates that there is a very real demand for automated resource sharing. Even a large and established resource sharing network, like ILLINET Online, however, has its limitations. For example, ILLINET Online interlibrary loan activity accounts for only a little more than a third of the interlibrary loan activity within Illinois in a given year.

While ILLINET Online is a single system accounting for one third of the activity, a large portion of the remaining two thirds of the requests are placed against the holdings of fourteen other automated systems in the state. The eighteen regional library systems operate fourteen Local Library System Automation Programs (LLSAPs). Thirteen of these systems are standalone systems representing a number of different library automation vendors. The fourteenth LLSAP (operated by the North Suburban Library System) is a group of disparate automated systems also representing a number of library automation vendors.

It has been estimated that the holdings count in the LLSAPs is roughly equal to the holdings count in ILLINET Online (approximately 20 million volumes). While there is some degree of overlap between the holdings represented in ILLINET Online and the holdings represented in the LLSAPs, there is also much diversity. ILLINET Online records are derived from the state's OCLC subscription tapes; many of the LLSAPs used vendors other than OCLC for their retrospective conversions. Many of the LLSAPs also have fairly detailed holdings information and circulation status for public, special, and school libraries; the detailed holdings information and circulation status in ILLINET Online mainly represents academic libraries.

In addition to the LLSAPs, there are other major automated systems in the state. Two major research libraries, Northwestern University and the University of Chicago, operate standalone systems. These systems together contain millions of records that are not represented in either ILLINET Online or the LLSAPs. Detailed holdings information and circulation status for these two institutions are likewise not represented.

Thus, in Illinois, a true union catalog would contain the holdings represented in more than twenty individual automated systems. While a true union catalog would give users access to an amazing wealth of resources, such a catalog for the entire state is an unlikely possibility for fiscal, technical, and political reasons. However unlikely a physical union catalog may be, a virtual union catalog is an achievable goal. The Linked Systems for Resource Sharing Project is an attempt to create a virtual union catalog for the state of Illinois.

LINKED SYSTEMS
FOR RESOURCE SHARING PROJECT

The University of Illinois received $35,000 in LSCA Title III funds in 1990 to begin investigating the feasibility of linking ILLI-NET Online with other disparate automated library systems in the state. During the first project year a preliminary plan was put together to guide the project in subsequent years. The primary goal of the project is to develop links between ILLINET Online, the fourteen LLSAPs, and the major standalones that are identified in the Illinois State Library's Plan for Funding Automated Resource Sharing in Illinois Libraries. The linking of these systems has been identified by the Illinois State Library as a major priority for funding at the state level.

The Plan outlines two basic criteria for the project. The interface must automatically route searching transactions from one system to the next and enable users to either initiate a circulation transaction or place a hold on an item. The interface must also serve as a user-friendly intermediary, using a common command language or translator, between the user and each major system, so that the user need not know the command language and search structures required by the individual systems.

Project participants also reviewed and endorsed a number of standards and protocols for potential use in conjunction with the project:

- International Standards Organization Open Systems Interconnection (ISO-OSI) Reference Model.
- American National Standards Institute (ANSI) Z39.50 (Information Retrieval Service Definition and Protocol Specification for Library Applications).
- ANSI Z39.58 (Common Command Language for Library Applications).

- TCP/IP Suite (Transmission Control Protocol and the Internet Protocol).
- ISO International Standard for Interlibrary Loan.

During the first year of the project, the Linked Systems for Resource Sharing Task Force served as a steering committee for the project. The Task Force dealt with two major issues: defining the procedural and political aspects of the project and preparing background information for project consultants, who will develop a detailed design document that will guide the actual implementation of the project in subsequent years.

The first procedural/political issue that the Task Force dealt with concerned physical access or connection to the network. Who can connect to the network? Who can initiate interlibrary loan transactions over the network? How will the links work?

In the early stages of discussion, the Task Force favored a strategy whereby each of the individual systems would use ILLINET Online as a communications hub. Each system would be capable of searching the database and routing interlibrary loan transactions to the libraries that owned the items. Conversely, ILLINET Online users could also search the system and be linked to items in other databases. The idea was to implement links between the various systems using ILLINET Online as a communications hub.

Ultimately, planning called for patron-initiated interlibrary loan transactions. Through this interconnection, patrons could use public access terminals on the disparate systems, or dial access, to connect to ILLINET Online to find records and to initiate requests for items without the intervention of a librarian.

Several basic guidelines were developed to govern the interlibrary loan process:

1. Local needs should take precedence over external needs.
2. Users should be encouraged to request items that are available (i.e., on the shelf). If an item is in circulation or otherwise unavailable at one library, users should be directed to locate an available copy at another library.
3. Standard terminology must be developed. Potentially confus-

ing terms, like "save," "reserve," "charge," etc., can have different meanings to users of different systems.

4. The Illinois Interlibrary Loan Code needs to be broadened to explicitly cover linked systems for resource sharing and interlibrary loans.

5. The Illinois Library Computer Systems Organization Interlibrary Borrowing Code needs to be modified to make explicit references to the use of ILLINET Online by patrons of other automated systems.

6. Procedures and guidelines should be formalized to cover the process of placing interlibrary loans through system-to-system links.

These preliminary guidelines have been the subject of considerable discussion, and formal guidelines for the project are approaching fruition. It now appears that the guiding philosophy may best be expressed as "exhaust local resources before going statewide."

Libraries should first search the LLSAP of the library system to which they belong to determine if the item in question is available locally. The next step will probably be to search the LLSAP of another library system that is "logically related" to the LLSAP of the searching library. This logical connection may be the geographic proximity of the LLSAPs, the use by two LLSAPs of the same vendor software, or the type of material requested. For example, perhaps an LLSAP has known collection strengths in the subject area of the search. The logical connection could also be a byproduct of document delivery effectiveness. Perhaps some library systems could be partners due to their locations on the statewide delivery service.

After local resources and logical connections were exhausted, the search could be directed to ILLINET Online to determine if the item had been cataloged by an OCLC library in Illinois. If the item were held by one of the forty ILLINET Online direct participants, a request could be placed at that time. If it were held by another library, the request would be directed to the LLSAP with which the library was affiliated.

Future directions for the Linked Systems for Resource Sharing Project will be determined over the course of 1992. Consultants have sent out a questionnaire to all participants. The purpose of the questionnaire is to try to develop a formal consensus in terms of policy directions, as well as to gather operational and technical information on the many systems involved. The consultants will use the information obtained from the questionnaire to develop a detailed design document. The purpose of this document will be to outline a set of specifications that any library or library system must observe in order to participate in this virtual union catalog.

CONCLUSION

The Linked Systems for Resource Sharing Project is a good example of how cooperative access to other library catalogs can work. Many of the policy questions and issues that the Task Force has dealt with can be seen to parallel the recent interest in Internet-accessible catalogs, with one important difference: the Linked Systems for Resource Sharing Project represents a truly multi-type approach to the sharing of library resources. Other system linking or remote access projects could benefit from studying the Linked Systems for Resource Sharing Project.

The Z39.50 Protocol:
An Implementor's Perspective

Mark H. Needleman

SUMMARY. This article describes the University of California MELVYL(R)[1] system and its implementation of the Z39.50 information retrieval protocol. It describes the protocol itself and the implementation of it that is being done as part of the UC MELVYL system. It also discusses some of the open issues involving the protocol as well as some of the activities that are going on in the implementation arena. Finally it attempts to discuss some of the implications of the Z39.50 protocol for the library and information world.

BACKGROUND

The Division of Library Automation (DLA) is administered by the Office of the Associate Vice President-Information Systems and Administrative Services within the office of the President of the University of California. DLA is charged with the management and

Mark H. Needleman is Coordinator of Advanced Technology Development for the Office of the President, Division of Library Automation, University of California, Kaiser Center Room 854, 300 Lakeside Drive, Oakland, CA 94612-3550 (Internet e-mail: mhn@stubbs.ucop.edu).

The author wishes to thank colleagues Bob Brandriff, Ellen England, Margery Tibbets, and Michael Thwaites at the University of California Office of the President for their ideas and input for this article and comments on the text itself. Many of the ideas expressed here come from papers on Z39.50 by Clifford Lynch (Director, University of California Office of the President, Division of Library Automation) and conversations with him. Much of the description of the Z39.50 protocol is adapted from his writings on the subject. Much of what is right and informative in this article is owed to others.

© 1992 by The Haworth Press, Inc. All rights reserved.

implementation of University-wide library automation activities. To this end, DLA provides bibliographic services that UC library patrons and others use to determine what library materials the university holds and where these materials are located in the over 100 libraries of the UC system and the California State Library. These Services include:

- The MELVYL Online Catalog
- The California Academic Libraries List of Serials (CALLS)
- MELVYL MEDLINE(R)[2]
- MELVYL Current Contents(R)[3]
- MELVYL Magazine Database
- MELVYL Newspaper Database
- MELVYL Computer Database(R)[4]

The MELVYL catalog contains records of UC's book and periodicals holdings as well as records of other materials such as maps and music scores. The catalog also includes the book holdings of the California State Library. The periodicals file (CALLS) includes the holdings of the University of California, Stanford University, the University of Southern California, the nineteen-campus California State University system, and selected other libraries. The MELVYL books database contains about 6.5 million records which represent approximately 13 million holdings. The CALLS periodical file contains about 815,000 records.

The MELVYL MEDLINE database, a joint project of DLA and the UC health sciences libraries, contains the current five year file of the National Library of Medicine MEDLINE database, which includes article citations and abstracts from over 4,000 health sciences journals. The database currently contains about 1.5 million records.

The MELVYL Current Contents database contains the table of contents of journals indexed by the Institute for Scientific Information (ISI). Currently there are approximately 1 million citations from about 6,500 journals.

The MELVYL Magazine database contains approximately 670,000 citations and abstracts from over 1000 periodicals indexed by Information Access Company. The periodicals covered are from the Expanded Academic Index(R)[5] and are primarily in the areas of humanities and social sciences.

The MELVYL Newspaper database contains about 650,000 newspaper citations from the New York Times, Washington Post, Los Angeles Times, Wall Street Journal and Christian Science Monitor indexed by Information Access Company. This data comes from the IAC National Newspaper Index(R).[6]

The MELVYL Computer database contains approximately 200,000 citations and abstracts from over 200 computer-related journals and magazines indexed by Information Access Company.

During the academic year the MELVYL system averages approximately 130,000 sessions per week. This activity represents about 450,000 searches per week with over 4 million records being displayed.

THE Z39.50 PROTOCOL

The Z39.50 protocol evolved out of work that had been done in the early 1980's called the Linked Systems Project (LSP). This project involved the Library of Congress, The Online Computer Library Center (OCLC), The Research Libraries Information Network (RLIN), and the Western Library Network (WLN). This project built a prototype network to transfer bibliographic records among these groups and developed a precursor to the Z39.50 protocol. In 1984 the protocol that was developed as part of the LSP project was turned over to the National Information Standards Organization (NISO), the ANSI-accredited standards development body, for further development and consideration as a U.S. national standard. Z39.50 Version 1 became a U.S. National standard in 1988.[7]

Work on information retrieval protocols was also going on in the international arena. There is an international standard protocol known as Search and Retrieval ISO 10162 (service definition) and ISO 10163 (protocol definition). Z39.50 Version 2 1992, which is currently out for ballot within NISO, brings the U.S. standard into alignment with the international standard. Z39.50 Version 2, if adopted, will essentially make the U.S. standard a superset of the international version.

The Z39.50 protocol provides a generalized mechanism for transmitting and managing queries and result sets using the client server model. Although it originally came out of the bibliographic and library world, there is nothing in the protocol that restricts its use to that type of data. In fact, the protocol is specifically designed to be a generalized mechanism that can be used with many and multiple types of data. The server is presumed to contain one or more databases that contain a series of objects called records. Each database contains a series of access points that the client can use to search, although not all databases may contain the same set of access points nor may all possible values for the access points be present in all records in a single database.

The searches that the client performs against the server create result sets. Records from these result sets can be presented to the client and/or combined with other searches to produce new result sets. It is also presumed that there are one or more common syntaxes that the client and server commonly understand that describe the format of the returned records. It is not presumed that the same syntax is shared in all databases on the server, although nothing prohibits this, nor is it presumed that all elements described by an individual syntax are present in all records returned to the client by the server.

An example of a record syntax that would be used for bibliographic data, for instance, is the MARC format. Also note that nothing in the protocol says anything at all about the organization or storage of the databases on the server itself. What is described is the mechanism for communication of searches and the presentation of results between the client and server.

The client and server communicate with each other through a series of Application Protocol Data Units (APDU). The Z39.50 protocol was originally specified as an OSI application layer protocol and assumes services on its behalf by some of the upper OSI layers. Much of the previous discussion about the knowledge of syntaxes, for example, is assumed to take place in the supporting OSI protocol stack. Most current Z39.50 implementations, however, are being done using TCP/IP.

The basic protocol interactions between the client and server are as follows. A client initiates a Z39.50 session with a server by means of an INITIALIZE request. The server responds with an INITIALIZE response. These APDU's are used for the client and server to set up commonly agreed upon parameters for the session. Once the session is established the client can send SEARCH requests to the server indicating the search the client wants performed. The server responds with a SEARCH response APDU indicating the success or failure of the request.

Only one SEARCH request can be outstanding at any given time. The SEARCH request specifies the name of the result set under which the resulting retrieved records are saved on the server. The server may or may not support the ability to save multiple result sets, but the protocol requires it to support saving at least a single result set for every search. If saving only one result set is supported, the server automatically overwrites any result set saved by a prior search. Otherwise the client can specify a name for a result set and whether the server should replace an older result set of the same name.

Transmission of records from a result set on the server back to the client is initiated by means of a PRESENT request, to which the server responds with a PRESENT response. Like the SEARCH request, only one PRESENT request can be outstanding at any given time. The server may require multiple PRESENT requests in order to transfer an entire result set. The size and number of records transmitted are both specified in the PRESENT request and controlled by parameters that were established during session initiation.

A facility exists for the client to dispose of result sets it has stored on the server. A DELETE request is used by the client to delete one or more (or all) of the result sets it has on the server. The status of the request is returned to the client by the server in a DELETE response APDU.

Currently there is no facility defined in the Z39.50 protocol to terminate a session. The protocol relies on lower layer services to perform that function and it is thus not possible to terminate a Z39.50 session while keeping the lower layer associations open.

In addition to these basic functions, in the U.S. standard, there are some mechanisms for the server to initiate communication with the client. A RESOURCE CONTROL request can be used by the server to inform the client, for example, that a particular search will take a long time, produce a large result set, or incur a significant cost. The server can request confirmation from the client to verify that the client wants to proceed anyway. The client can thus tell the server to continue with the search or to cancel it. There is also a mechanism for the client to ask the server to invoke RESOURCE CONTROL so that it can, for instance, find out how much a particular search has cost so far.

An ACCESS CONTROL request is a generalized mechanism for the server to challenge the client for a password or any other type of authentication. The client would respond to the challenge with an ACCESS CONTROL response. ACCESS CONTROL can be invoked by the server based on the database the client is attempting to search, a specific record being presented, or any other criteria. Multiple RESOURCE CONTROL request/RESOURCE CONTROL response and/or ACCESS CONTROL request/ACCESS CONTROL response sequences can occur while a single SEARCH, PRESENT, or other request is in progress. RESOURCE CONTROL and ACCESS CONTROL are present only in the U.S. standard. At the time of this publication they do not exist in the international version.

Several different query types are defined in the protocol. A Type 0 query is a mechanism that allows passing the search as a character text string. The protocol does not regulate the format of this string, which is established by prior agreement between the client and server. A Type 1 query is specified using Reverse Polish Notation (RPN).[8] Support for the Common Command Language in both the U.S. and international versions is also incorporated into the protocol. Support for the Type 1 query is mandatory for conformance to the protocol.

An attribute set for searching bibliographic data is specified in the protocol. The attribute set contains access points such as Name, Title, ISBN, etc., that can be used to search databases. Also contained in the attribute set are relational attributes such as GREATER THAN or EQUAL, and structure attributes such as access point is a word or access point is a list of words. Boolean operators such as AND, OR, and ANDNOT can also be used to combine results using multiple sets of attributes. An error message set is also defined in support of this attribute set.

Although currently only one attribute set (i.e., the one in support of bibliographic data) is defined in the standard, it is expected both that this attribute set will be used for non-bibliographic data where appropriate, and that other attribute sets for other types of data will be defined and registered as the protocol achieves more widespread use among many different types of databases. The Library of Congress (LC) is the maintenance agency for Z39.50, and in that role, acts as the registration authority for things that get registered in support of the protocol (e.g., attribute sets). LC will also maintain a list of registered implementors of the protocol.

THE MELVYL SYSTEM Z39.50 IMPLEMENTATION

In 1990 the University of California Office of the President received a grant from Digital Equipment Corporation to link the UC MELVYL system to Penn State's LIAS system using Z39.50. Work on this project began in 1991 and phase one of the project is approaching completion at the time of this publication. We have successfully linked MELVYL, in both client and server modes, to Penn State, Data Research Associates, and the University of California at Berkeley. Other implementations will be tested as they become available.

Currently only the main bibliographic database is supported by the implementation. Work will now go forward in phase two to upgrade the code, add support for additional databases, and add new features. We also plan to begin a project with the University of California at Davis and DRA to link the MELVYL system to a DRA system recently installed at Davis. The goal is to link the bibliographic records in the MELVYL system to the circulation records in the DRA system using Z39.50 so that a user displaying Davis records on the MELVYL system will be able to see the current circulation status of those items as retrieved from the DRA system. This project demonstrates another application for the Z39.50 protocol beyond the original bibliographic environment from which it developed and to which some people still relegate the protocol.

The MELVYL software runs on an IBM mainframe computer. Most of the MELVYL user interface software is written in PL/1. The database management software used by the MELVYL system, as well as the communications and networking software supporting it, however, are written in IBM assembler language. The Z39.50 implementation consists of three components: client software, server software, and the protocol machinery program.

The client supports MELVYL system users who want to access a remote system. The client code exists as part of the MELVYL software itself. To a MELVYL system user a remote Z39.50 database appears as if it were just one more locally mounted database that can be selected. Most of the normal MELVYL system commands, such as FIND and DISPLAY, are supported. The MELVYL interface software translates the user's commands into Z39.50 APDU's and forwards them on to the remote server for processing. It then takes the results sent back from the remote server and presents them to the user in the familiar MELVYL system format.

The server supports users from remote systems who wish to access the MELVYL system. It exists as a separate PL/1 program that listens on the network for incoming Z39.50 sessions. It takes those requests and maps them into user commands that it passes on to the MELVYL system to be executed. It then takes the MELVYL system responses, packages them up, and sends them back out to the remote site. Since the MELVYL software recognizes that it is dealing with the server program, the data it returns are streamlined in such a way that they are more easily handled by the server.

Both the MELVYL client and the server program rely on a third component, the Z39.50 protocol machinery program, for handling the Z39.50 APDU's and for dealing with the underlying networking software. Written in IBM assembler language, this component provides the interfaces between the MELVYL client and the network on the one hand, and the network and the server program on the other. The underlying networking protocols are TCP/IP.

In the current MELVYL system architecture the user interface and the database retrieval engine are closely linked together. Plans call for upgrading the MELVYL system design to separate those functions into a true client/server model. Under the upgraded design, the client interfaces, for both regular terminals and graphical interfaces, will use Z39.50 as the underlying retrieval mechanism. The server program will also be changed to a true database server. The current server program just maps Z39.50 requests into MEL-VYL system commands for execution as if typed directly by a user.

Being one of the earliest implementors of the Z39.50 protocol, we gained an interesting perspective on the process of implementing such a protocol. The Z39.50 specification does not address all of the details and remains open to interpretation in some areas. One must choose which options an implementation will support, how to handle options passed by remote users that are not supported locally, and how to pick appropriate buffer and record sizes. The fact that two systems support the Z39.50 protocol does not necessarily mean that they will interoperate, or that, even if they do interoperate at a protocol level, meaningful data can be exchanged.

One of the more interesting decisions for an implementor is how to produce Z39.50 queries that will be understood by a remote system. Currently, there is nothing in the protocol itself (except for a defined search attribute set, record transfer syntax, and error message set) to help in making this decision. At the time of this publication, almost all of these issues require mechanisms that are outside the protocol and prior agreements among the systems involved. Work progresses to help alleviate this situation.

A client must know what indexes are supported by various databases on a server and what attributes, and combination of attributes, can be used to access these indexes. The client also must know how the Z39.50 search attributes are mapped to local indexes by the server and what the server will do with attributes it does not support or may interpret differently than the client may have intended. For example, the author index on one system may be radically different from the author index on another system, and different again from the way the client searches authors on its local system. Likewise, the server must be able to take incoming search attributes and map them to searches that make sense and are valid within its databases.

Another area in which congruence between client and server arises is in error handling. The MELVYL system has a large set of error messages it can return to local users. These messages must be mapped into the substantially smaller set of Z39.50 error messages currently defined for bibliographic data. Thus, an implementor decides how best to do that mapping so as to provide error handling to a remote user within the constraints allowed.

Early implementors had to make common decisions about these issues in order to have various implementations interoperate. More experience with the protocol and wider implementation will undoubtedly lead to reevaluation of these agreements over time.

OTHER IMPLEMENTATIONS AND ACTIVITIES

Several other Z39.50 implementations are currently in place or under development. In the library community, the Library of Congress, OCLC, RLG, and Data Research Associates are all working on Z39.50. NOTIS Systems has recently announced their NOTIS to NOTIS link (PACLink) using a variation of the protocol. They intend to make PACLink fully compliant so that it will link to non-NOTIS systems as well. Penn State is involved in a joint Z39.50 project with the UC MELVYL system, and the Florida Center for Library Automation is working on Z39.50 for their NOTIS system as well.

The University of California at Berkeley is working on a campus information system that will incorporate Z39.50. This project extends the use of the protocol to include full-text and non-bibliographic data. The WAIS (Wide-Area Information Server) project is upgrading their software to be fully compliant with Z39.50 version 2–demonstrating the applicability of the protocol to full-text document retrieval. There are a growing number of implementations; even more will emerge in the coming year.

Z39.50 IMPLEMENTOR ORGANIZATIONS

In 1990 the Z39.50 Implementors Group (ZIG) was formed by representatives of organizations in the United States that were working on or planning Z39.50 implementations. The membership of this group has steadily increased as new organizations move forward with their implementations. While the original focus of this group was on interoperability, it has broadened its scope to include proposals for enhancements to the protocol itself. For example, participants developed an EXPLAIN facility that would allow a standardized way for a client to find out characteristics of a server, including what databases it supports, which attributes those databases support for searching, and other important characteristics about the server. Currently a client cannot get this information except through a priori knowledge of an individual server. As the number of servers grows, collecting this server information will become an increasingly unworkable situation.

Other work done by the group includes proposals for handling result sets that would persist beyond an individual session, a BROWSE facility for browsing databases as opposed to searching them, new attribute sets for different types of data such as financial and news-oriented data, and a SORT facility to sort the records in a result set by various criteria. Early on the group agreed to use a mechanism for handling experimental extensions to the protocol as a way to gain experience with something new. If the experiment were to succeed, the proposed extension would then be fed back into the standards process to be incorporated in a later revision of Z39.50.

The ZIG maintains an anonymous FTP server at think.com (a computer operated by the staff of Thinking Machines Corporation), where electronic versions of many of its documents are housed and can be retrieved.[9] It also runs a LISTSERV mailing list that is publicly open to any interested party. The mailing list address is:

Z3950IW@NERVM.BITNET (BITNET)
or
Z3950IW@nervm.nerdc.ufl.edu (Internet)

Normal LISTSERV mechanisms and facilities are used with this list for subscribing and getting mail.

Another important and exciting development is the Z39.50 Interoperability Testbed Project sponsored by the Coalition for Networked Information (CNI). The participating organizations are committed to implementing Z39.50 over TCP/IP. They have agreed to implement a compliant client and/or server based on specifications that will be developed by the testbed project. Within six months of the finalization of those specifications, they agree to make their implementation available over the Internet for interoperability testing by other project members. Participants have also agreed to commit whatever resources are needed to accomplish this goal.

Z39.50 is an OSI application layer protocol. As such, it relies on lower-level OSI services that are not present in the TCP/IP protocol suite. One of the major goals of the CNI testbed will be to build consensus on which of those services need to be incorporated into the TCP/IP environment and how to stage those services in a consistent manner among all implementations. The specifications developed by the testbed project will be public documents, and, after they have been validated by real-world experience, they will be fed back into the standards process.

While the Z39.50 Implementors Group includes members who are implementing Z39.50 in many different ways, as well as some who are in the planning or awareness stages, the CNI Interoperability Testbed project is limited to a focused group of organizations developing real-world interoperable systems in a very limited time-frame. The intent is to demonstrate interoperability among the project members by the summer of 1992. Among the members of the testbed project are the University of California Office of the President, the University of California at Berkeley, the University of Washington, Apple Computer, Pennsylvania State University, Thinking Machines Corporation, CARL Systems, Stanford University, Data Research Associates, Mead Data, and VTLS.

THE FUTURE

This is an exciting and dynamic time for the Z39.50 protocol. Although it has been a U.S. national standard for several years, real-world implementations are just now beginning to appear. Based on our experience at DLA and my personal observations, I expect the following developments to occur over the next couple of years.

More compliant servers will appear. The CNI testbed project will promote this development. The early core of servers available now will influence the development of new implementations. Some of the interoperability agreements that will be worked out as part of the testbed projects, as well as the lessons learned in these early implementations, will set standards for new developers who will benefit greatly from the problems solved by early pioneers. By avoiding much of the "fumbling in the dark" of the pioneers, these new players will be able to bring their implementations online more quickly. The core of early servers will also provide a ready testbed against which new developers may debug their implementations.

Clients will proliferate, many of them free and publicly available, for all sorts of hardware platforms and operating environments. Implementations will exist for everything from mainframe computers through Unix workstations and down to IBM personal computers and Apple Macintoshes. All popular operating systems and environments, such as DOS, OS/2, and Windows, will be supported. Z39.50 will be incorporated into the user interfaces of many different types of systems, including graphical user interfaces, both inside and outside the library world. In many cases, the user will still see the graphical interface, but the underlying mechanism for accessing data will become Z39.50. The WAIS project will play an important role in this area.

Z39.50 will be used for new types of applications and new types of data that go far beyond the traditional environment of bibliographic data from which it first emerged. Use with non-bibliographic and non-library data has already begun and will continue to increase. Attribute sets for searching and transfer syntaxes will be developed for a wide range of different types of data and will be used with a wide range of different applications. Such developments will finally put to rest the mistaken belief that Z39.50 is just a library protocol with no wider applicability.

Over the next couple of years many of the extensions developed by groups such as the Z39.50 Implementors Group will make their appearance in real-world implementations. Implementors will experiment and refine these extensions. This work will also more clearly define the future of the protocol, thereby enhancing the functionality and usability of it. Many developments have yet to be imagined.

CONCLUSION

This article provides an overview of the UC MELVYL system, the Z39.50 protocol itself, and the role of that protocol in the MELVYL system. It also examines some of the other activities surrounding Z39.50 and some developments that are beginning to emerge. This is an exciting and revolutionary period in the information retrieval world. Z39.50 is likely to be a major building block in developments currently underway and emerging. This protocol makes possible the development of network-based information resources and a shift in paradigm from traditional perceptions about information and information resources to ones yet undefined. To use a protocol like Z39.50 and not begin to make that conceptual leap negates the reasons for developing it in the first place.

NOTES

1. MELVYL is a registered trademark of the Regents of The University of California.

2. MEDLINE is a registered trademark of the National Library of Medicine.

3. Current Contents is a registered trademark of the Institute for Scientific Information.

4. Computer Database is a registered trademark of Information Access Corporation.

5. Expanded Academic Index is a registered trademark of Information Access Corporation.

6. National Newspaper Index is a registered trademark of Information Access Corporation.

7. For details on the early history of the protocol, see Lynch and Preston (1990).

8. Reverse Polish Notation (RPN) is a method of forming mathematical expressions in which each operator is preceded by its operands and indicates the operation to be performed on the operands or the intermediate results that precede

it. (Rosenberg, *Dictionary of Computers, Information Processing, and Telecommunications*, 1987.)

9. To retrieve these documents from this FTP site, the reader must have access to the Internet. Contact local computing support personnel for questions regarding these capabilities.

BIBLIOGRAPHY

International Organization for Standardization (ISO). *Documentation–Search and Retrieve Service Definition*. ISO/TC46/SC4/WG4. ISO/IS 10162. Vienna, VA: Omnicom, 1990. Available from Omnicom Information Service, 115 Park St., SE, Vienna, VA 22180.

International Organization for Standardization (ISO). *Documentation–Search and Retrieve Protocol Specification*. ISO/TC46/SC4/WG4. ISO/IS 10163. Vienna, VA: Omnicom, 1990. Available from Omnicom Information Service, 115 Park St., SE, Vienna, VA 22180.

Lynch, Clifford A. "Information Retrieval as Network Application." *Library Hi-Tech* 8, no. 4 (1990): 59-74.

Lynch, Clifford A. "The Z39.50 Information Retrieval Protocol: An Overview and Status Report." *Computer Communication Review* 21, no. 1 (January 1991): 55-70.

Lynch, Clifford A. "The Z39.50 Protocol: Questions and Answers." Data Research Associates.

Lynch, Clifford A., and Cecilia M. Preston. "Internet Access to Information Resources." *Annual Review of Information Science and Technology* 25 (1990): 263-312.

McGill, Michael J. "Z39.50 Benefits for Designers and Users." *EDUCOM Review* 24, no. 3 (Fall 1989): 27-30.

National Information Standards Organization. *American National Standard Z39.50, Information Retrieval Service Definition and Protocol Specifications for Library Applications*. New Brunswick, NJ: Transaction Publishers, 1988.

Internetworking:
New Opportunities and Challenges in Resource Sharing

Craig A. Summerhill

SUMMARY. This article focuses on the impact internetworking is having upon academic research libraries with special emphasis given to collection development and resource sharing in an electronically networked environment. A brief history of the Internet, NSF-Net, and NREN is given. Genres of information resources currently existing on the network and future trends in the development of electronic libraries are discussed.

A BRIEF INTERNETWORKING HISTORY

The Internet

In 1968, the Department of Defense Advanced Research Projects Agency Network (ARPANet or DARPANet), an experimental packet switching network, was introduced (Quarterman 1990, 143). This network, which used leased lines to link academic institutions, defense contractors, and other government researchers, was designed around the TCP/IP (Transmission Control Protocol/Internet Protocol) suite of protocols. From the creation of the TCP/IP

Craig A. Summerhill is Systems Coordinator at the Coalition for Networked Information, 1527 New Hampshire Avenue, N.W., Washington, DC 20036 (Internet e-mail: craig@cni.org).

The Coalition for Networked Information is a joint project of the Association of Research Libraries, CAUSE, and EDUCOM, formed in 1990 to promote the creation of and access to information resources in networked environments in order to enrich scholarship and enhance intellectual productivity.

© 1992 by The Haworth Press, Inc. All rights reserved.

protocol suite was born the term "inter-networking," a term which refers to the ability of disparate computers–computers designed with differing hardware architectures and running differing operating systems–to inter-operate. The term "Internet" with a capital "I" refers specifically to the DARPA Internet.

The NSFNet

The National Science Foundation (NSF) established six national supercomputing centers in 1984. In order to provide researchers with better access to these resources, NSF initiated a program to link these computing centers via a network called NSFNet. Since the Open Systems Interconnection standard (OSI) was not widely available, NSF adopted the TCP/IP protocol suite for use on NSFNet. NSFNet was built upon a three tiered network topology: (1) a national backbone consisting of switching hubs in NSF supercomputing sites, (2) regional (mid-level) networks linking municipalities and organizations in like geographic regions of the country to the NSFNet backbone sites, and (3) local area networks linking individual organizations (universities, colleges, military sites, businesses) to the national network via the mid-level regionals.

As computing professionals and academic librarians alike will testify, the past five years has been a period of unprecedented growth for packet switched networking in general, and for the Internet in particular. This growth is largely a result of the successes of MERIT Computing, Inc., a Michigan based educational computing consortium. In 1987, MERIT received a grant from the National Science Foundation to expand and re-engineer the NSFNet backbone. Since that time, the Internet has expanded at such a tremendous rate that it is not possible to calculate the exact number of computers currently connected to the network.

In January, 1992, the Network Information Center of the Department of Defense Network released a Request for Comment (RFC) regarding the number of hosts on the current network (Lottor 1992). RFC1296 speculates that there are in excess of 800,000 individual computers connected to the Internet at this time. Regardless of the exact number of hosts on the network, it is clear that network traffic has increased over the past five years. Network traffic patterns increased at a rate of twenty percent per month in the years immediately following the awarding of the 1987 MERIT contract. By September 1991, the resulting growth in network traffic led to the introduction of random sampling in the data gathering procedures used for the compilation of monthly NSF statistics.

The National Research and Education Network (NREN)

On December 9, 1991 President Bush signed into law the National High Performance Computing Act of 1991 (P.L. 102-194). The signing of the NREN bill brought to fruition several years of intensive effort on the part of the higher education community, computing professionals, and librarians to ensure the passage of legislation designed to develop a national information superhighway–an omnipresent electronic network designed to internetwork universities, research institutions, businesses, public libraries, and public schools.

Originally introduced in 1988 by Senator Albert Gore as S. 1067 (McClure 1990, 16-17), the National High Performance Computing Act as it was signed into law authorizes the creation of the National Research and Education Network (NREN), and calls for additional government funded research and development in advanced computing applications. Although this authorization to appropriate funding is a significant step toward the creation of a nationally ubiquitous information delivery medium, many significant obstacles persist in the fulfillment of this vision. These barriers, ranging from local to federal in scope, are administrative, economic, ethical, legal, and social in nature.

As the NREN does not yet physically exist, the term "interim inter-agency NREN" is increasingly being used to refer to the existing Internet. Members of the existing interim inter-agency networking community have already overcome many barriers preventing the development of such a nationally accessible network. Others are actively engaged in programs and research to find solutions to remaining barriers–solutions which are mutually acceptable by all parties having a vested interest in NREN development.

Librarians constitute one of the groups of academic professionals most active in ensuring the development of the NREN. The reasons for the library community's involvement are self-evident. Electronic networking offers new methods of delivering information to existing library clientele, and it will create new jobs for librarians well versed in internetworking technologies. In addition, networking presents new challenges and frontiers in librarianship, and it offers alternative solutions to existing problems such as the skyrocketing cost of journal subscriptions.

Why the NREN?

An inevitable question arises, why the NREN? Why build a new network instead of utilizing an existing library bibliographic network for providing a ubiquitous information delivery medium? The answers are clear. People (i.e., users) would have access to the new network, and a large infrastructure is already developed in the form of the Internet. Secondly, current users appear to enjoy interacting with the network. Thirdly, the network is robust and reliable.

Larsen notes that in order for networked information delivery to thrive, it is necessary to have a carrier capable of reaching the homes and offices of the library users and equally capable of reaching the offices of librarians and the existing library networks they use.

> One clear need is for libraries and their suppliers to offer more of their services over a common network, accessible to the patron. The Internet is the obvious choice for academic libraries in higher education, and if the intent of the NREN initiative is met, then this may well become the choice of preference for other libraries as well. (1991, 42-42)

ARPANet was originally envisioned to be a network which would be used to link supercomputers and highly specialized scientific equipment. By linking these resources, large scientific datasets could be more readily shared and the expensive investment in scientific equipment could be amortized across a larger potential user group thus reducing costs to all users. Almost as soon as the network began functioning, however, researchers began using the network for electronic communication (Quarterman 1990, 144).

By 1987, when MERIT began re-engineering the NSFNet backbone, a growing user community primed for the delivery of electronic information already existed. Certainly, growth in network traffic is due as much to the fact that there is a growing audience prepared to receive and process electronic data disseminated on the network, as it is due to the fact that humans are inherently social creatures. People like using the network.

The interim inter-agency NREN, the Internet, has proven to be a highly reliable network, despite the fact that existing session layer applications are somewhat barbaric.[1] Simple Mail Transfer Protocol (SMTP), File Transfer Protocol (FTP), and a virtual terminal emulation protocol (TELNET) are currently the most heavily used. This heavy use is more likely due to their wide availability (i.e., these protocols are in the public domain and based upon an openly published protocol standard, TCP/IP) than their worth as applications. Nevertheless, these limited applications are effective and reliable, and they have proven to be reasonably accessible to the end user. Although significant expansion of the network is likely to be hampered by the technical shortcomings of the TCP/IP protocol suite, the network is suitably stable to maintain a production environment while migration strategies aimed at moving the network toward an increasingly sophisticated level of operation can be designed and implemented.

EXISTING INFORMATION RESOURCES ON THE INTERNET

A Typology of Internet-Accessible Databases

A wealth of information resources already exists on the Internet. No single source adequately describes all of these resources. Many efforts, however, are now underway, by librarians and non-librarians alike, to enhance intellectual access to information resources on the network. One of the most ambitious, and perhaps most formally organized, of these efforts is the TopNode project of the Coalition for Networked Information, Working Group on Directories and Resource Information Services.[2] Through the TopNode project, the Coalition hopes to stimulate the creation of, and long-term maintenance of, a top-level database that guides the user to a variety of informational resources on the network.

It is beyond the scope of this paper to attempt to present all of the information resources currently available on the network. In fact, it may not even be possible. A brief overview of several differing genres of Internet databases, however, is in order. Existing Internet resources include the online public access catalogs (OPACs) of many libraries both in the United States and abroad, commercial databases, social service and public information databases, discipline-specific databases, and network information databases. The majority of these resources are accessible to all users of the network community.

The Online Public Access Catalog

In his article about connecting OPACs to the Internet, Lynch notes:

> Historically, library catalogs have been rather insular, often based on specialized hardware and/or operating systems lacking industry-standard networking capabilities. Network access was not a major consideration in the design or selection of these specialized systems. (1989, 7)

Although network implementations may not always be optimal, a growing number of online public access catalogs are becoming available on the Internet. For users wishing to search the contents of these databases, there are two major listings of these resources available on the network. Art St. George (University of New Mexico) and Ronald Larsen (University of Maryland) maintain a listing of over 100 such OPACs and other accessible databases.[3] A similar list is maintained by Billy Barron (University of North Texas).[4]

More than one member of the networking community has raised questions regarding the usefulness of Internet OPAC connections. On some electronic discussion lists, there has been considerable dialogue regarding access to OPACs via the Internet.[5] How useful is it to search a database of bibliographic citations when there is no immediate mechanism in place for delivering the actual material to the user? In August 1991, the Machine-Assisted Reference Section of the American Library Association, Reference and Adult Services Division (RASD/MARS) published *Library Resources on the Internet: Strategies for Selection and Use*. Several supporting arguments are made for the searching of Internet OPACs (Machine-Assisted Reference Section 1991, 11-12). Nevertheless, it seems apparent that a significant portion of the network community feels that their information needs are not met by searching OPACs.

Commercial Databases

As commercial databases became increasingly cost-effective to access and search, libraries began providing mediated database search services through providers such as DIALOG and BRS. Throughout the last decade, university libraries nationwide have begun to build localized versions of these heavily used commercial bibliographic databases by leasing the machine readable data files and loading them into local search systems. Accordingly, automated system vendors have modified their existing OPACs to accommodate multiple bibliographic databases (e.g., NOTIS Systems, Inc. through the MDAS release).

No uniform licensing arrangement for this type of supplemental machine-readable data file exists.[6] Licenses for use are most often negotiated on a case-by-case basis. Licensing fees for these resources are sometimes based upon the number of full-time equivalent students and/or employees present, or upon the number of simultaneous users that can access the database, or in rarer instances a flat fee for unlimited use can be negotiated. One result of the lack of uniform licensing is that individual implementations of these types of machine-readable data files vary greatly from site to site on the Internet.

The advent of internetworking has tremendously complicated the negotiation of licenses for these commercial products because open network access to library databases is viewed as a violation of licensing agreements by most providers of machine-readable data files. Subsequently, security of data and authentication of users have become critical issues in the design and implementation of networked library systems (Lynch 1989, 15-17). In order to comply with the licensing agreement for a commercial product, many library systems now need to make intelligent decisions about the origin of the terminal session before allowing access to certain databases. To complicate matters, many libraries must limit access to some databases while at the same time providing unlimited, open access to other databases on the same system.

Social Services/Public Information Databases

One of the chief strengths of the Internet, or any electronic network for that matter, is its ability to overcome the need for geographic proximity between the data and the user. In a traditional library, it is necessary for the client to enter the building to use resources which are physically housed within. The realm of the "virtual library," however, is one in which the user can enter the library from any location that can support a network connection–the home, the office, the classroom, a hotel room, or from another country. Indeed, it is quite common that the user will not even know where a database (and the computer it is mounted on) physically resides.

Ironically, databases of local community information are becoming increasingly popular on the Internet. These community information databases contain data on a wide variety of topics, such as campus sporting events, directory information for individuals affiliated with the local institution (i.e., white pages), collections of recipes, local job announcements, and electronic want ads. While it is not necessary to share geographic proximity with these resources in order to access them, the type of data contained within these systems is often most useful to people located in the community where the database is located.

Community information databases have developed simultaneously in the academic community and in our nation's municipalities. The term "Campus Wide Information System" (CWIS) is often used to refer to these services in the academic environment. The Cleveland Free-Net, a community information network run jointly by

Case Western Reserve University and public volunteers, is likely the largest municipal community information system accessible via the Internet. In five years of operation, the Cleveland Free-Net has been such a success that a not-for-profit corporation, the National Public Telecomputing Network, was created to promote the formation of community computing networks in other cities. At the time of this publication, systems with Internet connections exist in Cleveland, Ohio; Peoria, Illinois; Youngstown, Ohio; Medina County, Ohio; and Cincinnati, Ohio. Both Santa Barbara, California and Portland, Oregon are nearing the implementation of such systems, and there are nearly twenty other cities where organizing committees have been formed to investigate the topic (Delzeit 1992).

Discipline-Specific Databases

Discipline-specific databases on the network are a natural extension of scholarly research and communication. For the same reasons librarians have openly embraced computing systems–the ability to store and manipulate large quantities of data, the availability of enhanced data retrieval tools, and (through networks) the ability to have global access to data–scholars in many disciplines today are using machine-readable data in their personal research and publication. In fact, scholars may even be facing pressure to use automated tools in order to increase productivity and compete more effectively for research funding. Additionally, the desktop processing power available today makes it possible to work with data in ways that were considered impossible five to ten years ago. As a result of this increased computer use, scholars are amassing large personal collections of machine-readable data.

Occasionally, these data are organized, but often they are unstructured (i.e., "raw"), especially for researchers working in scientific fields. Some members of academe advocate a new role for libraries in the management of this raw data. Lucier (1990) and Matheson et al. (1989) have received considerable attention in the medical community for their efforts in the development of the Human Genome Data Base at Johns Hopkins University. The knowledge management theory advocates a re-positioning of libraries within the publication cycle. Rather than remaining passive consumers of pre-packaged data, Lucier believes that librarians can enhance access to raw data by organizing it and designing information systems to meet the specific needs of researchers as they arise.

Obviously, this type of service requires a considerable investment of time, energy, and resources in order to be successful. Lucier feels such an investment is justified, and that the mutual responsibility for knowledge management shared by scholars, scientists, and research librarians offers new opportunities for collaboration in academe. As a result of such partnerships, a variety of new informational resources can be created.

Databases About the Network

Perhaps, this genre of network resource is actually a subset of discipline-specific databases. If this is the case, then these databases constitute the most comprehensive collections of discipline-related data in existence on the network. Databases pertaining to computer hardware and software, networking protocols and standards, and electronic communication abound.

As librarians are fully aware, the compilation of a database can be a time consuming and costly undertaking. On the one hand, the keying of data is by far the most expensive element in the creation of any database, followed closely by the markup of data for inclusion in the actual database, and on-going maintenance of the system. On the other hand, databases that can be created from pre-existing collections of machine-readable data are extremely cost-effective by comparison. This type of data, which originates directly from the electronic pens and pads of network users, is generated in a thoroughly distributed environment. Each writer generates his or her own machine-readable copy.

Although questions regarding the quality of such databases exist–a significant amount of marginal material resides in many of these databases, one who has accessed them will quickly defend their usefulness. The skilled network navigator can weed from these living data collections bibliographic citations to both books and journal articles, citations to other useful network resources, and prose records of varying length covering a wide variety of computing and networking topics. If all attempts at solving one's quandary fail using these resources, one can always resort to posting a query to an electronic discussion list and thereby tap into the network's greatest asset, other users.

To some degree, the people at DARPA were correct in assuming that the network would lead to the sharing of datasets. The majority of shared data, however, is not the weighty scientific type as they envisioned, but is that which is most intellectually accessible to the majority of network users. While NASA astronomical datasets have a relatively limited audience, a database created from the archives of the Info-Mac Digest caters to a much wider audience. Assuming one possesses the skills and resources to access it, any person in the network community who works with Macintosh computers can benefit from this collection of data. Compiled over time, and archived for posterity and subsequent retrieval, these data have proven to be a useful resource for many Macintosh owners.[7]

INTERNETWORKING AND COLLECTION DEVELOPMENT

The User Community

Gardner notes the importance of collection development to the library and the librarian:

> The selection of materials for a collection is one of the essential parts of a librarian's job and also one of the most creative and interesting. The quality of the resulting collection is undoubtedly one of the criteria on which a librarian is most often judged. Users may not consciously always make such judgements, but if the collection fails to supply the information they need, they will certainly make an unconscious judgement and go elsewhere. (1981, xi)

Are libraries on the Internet providing the information resources which are most needed by the clientele? Are libraries providing an adequate level of access to the resources that are available on the network? If not, and Gardner is correct, these users will go elsewhere to meet their information needs.

Selectivity and Comprehensiveness

In an age of expanding information, libraries are faced with the realization that it is impossible, regardless of local financial endowment, to collect all materials that may be needed by the local user community. Therefore, the librarian must make decisions regarding the appropriateness of materials for inclusion in the local collection. This process is called collection development. When librarians engage in collection development, the goal is to retain within the library collection materials which most appropriately match the needs of the user community. In research libraries, the collection of materials which will build a comprehensive collection in a given subject area is also extremely important.

Even in a networked information environment such as the Internet, it seems evident that libraries will need to continue making collection development decisions. It is not possible, nor is it necessarily desirable, to mount all potentially useful electronic databases for use on a local system. Remote host performance constraints may warrant local installation of certain electronic resources rather than relying upon network connections to access the data. Electronic resources that are used by a relatively small portion of the local user community, however, are more likely candidates for network access.

Additionally, as new electronic resources appear, librarians need to be prepared to make difficult decisions about which resources the library will officially support. Currently, the number of electronic databases suitable for use in academic research libraries is relatively small. But their numbers are growing rapidly, and libraries will be forced to make decisions between comparable electronic resources. In system interface design, an argument can be made that databases listed on the second screen of the system menu are relegated a position of lesser importance. What criteria are used in determining the resources the library considers of primary importance and those considered of secondary importance? Critical examination of networked resources is required in order to make intelligent decisions regarding their suitability for use. Libraries must be able to justify these collection development decisions.

Gardner outlines several criteria which should be considered when making a determination of which materials to retain within the local collection: the authoritative nature of the work, the accuracy of the information presented, the impartiality of the work, recency of data, scope, depth of coverage, relevancy to the local user's condition, and cost (1981, 185-186). Katz lists a similar set of elements to be considered during the collection development process (1980, 91-96).

Obviously these types of criteria need to be considered when examining network resources–on the surface, they appear highly appropriate for use in examining electronic resources. There are several criteria, however, which are often used by the library profession that lose their relevancy when applied to electronic data. For example, the physical characteristics of books and journals such as typeface, quality of the paper, strength of binding, and the inclusion of bibliographies and indices are clearly not applicable to machine-readable data. Librarians, however, need to be aware of other unique characteristics of electronic data resources such as operating system dependencies, application software requirements, database storage requirements, and local processing constraints which need to be considered before attempting to retain a database for local use. Clearly, there is a need for academic librarians to redefine collection development criteria as they relate to networked information resources.

THE IMPACT OF INTERNETWORKING
ON RESOURCE SHARING

Transformation of the Academic Community

As an organization, the library derives its very existence from the socially accepted belief that collections of reading and research materials can be centrally managed in a manner that will adequately serve the information needs of all members of the community. In order to adequately serve those needs in an increasingly complex technological environment such as the Internet, it is mandatory that the library staff achieve and maintain technical skills at least as sophisticated as those members of the research community they hope to serve.

Although internetworking is not likely to change the essence of academic libraries–they will retain a central mission within the institution of serving the campus community's research and teaching needs, it seems evident that the manner in which this mission is met will evolve as a result of internetworking. Job descriptions and tasks within the academic library will need to change accordingly. New skills will be required, and new tasks will need to be accomplished.

Given the current network climate, it seems possible to make some reasonable projections about the form these changes will take:

- The academic community will continue to process information in an increasingly sophisticated manner using increasingly sophisticated computerized tools.
- The methods of data management currently employed by librarians will change.
- In order to serve the information needs of academe, the structure and content of library databases will change.
- The existing model of inter-library lending will be radically altered by the existence of wide area information servers.

Data Management and Library Staff

Graham (May 1990) has written about the effect the coming era of electronic communication will have upon technical services units in research libraries. He reports that there are four courses of action that technical services staff can choose to take in the coming period of network growth. They can choose to ignore it, and thereby relegate the research library to a role of increasingly smaller importance in the provision of information to the campus community. Or they can react by expanding access to electronic databases while continuing to maintain existing paper collections. The third choice involves the development of interfaces to integrate access to existing systems. Finally, the preservation of knowledge can become the responsibility of the library through the technical services staff.

Each of these options presents an increasingly complex set of challenges for the research library. The latter two, more innovative, models that Graham outlines require technological skills significantly more advanced than those required in the first two models. These higher levels of technological skills will have to be maintained and even continue to grow over time.

Providing public service in the networked environment will require a set of new skills also. Serving the information needs of remote library users is going to require the use of new tools, and use of existing tools such as electronic mail in a more effective manner. Someday technology will undoubtedly allow the realization of the "virtual reference desk" using two way video transmission on the network. In the interim period, however, alternative models of public service that do not resemble a drop-in reference desk need to be developed.

Rosenthal writes:

> If libraries are to provide acceptable levels of instruction and assistance to users, they must first devise and implement ongoing training programs for their staff members. In large research or public libraries this entails a variety of programs rather than a single training module. (1991, 14)

The larger the library, the more costly the training program, although staff training costs will vary from institution to institution just as existing levels of knowledge among the staff already vary widely. If library managers choose to ignore staff training needs, however, the costs to the library will be much greater. Despite the complexity of the task, there is a definite need within the profession to delineate a set of minimum technical skills needed by library professionals. Additionally, minimum technical skill guidelines for non-professional staff in research libraries should be re-evaluated. Defining computer literacy is not easy, and any change that affects people's lives and jobs is difficult to implement. This topic has caused and will continue to cause considerable disagreement among professionals. As the information environment becomes increasingly complex, however, the need for these skills becomes imperative.

The Evolving Library Database

Clearly, one of the lessons to be learned from the rapid growth of the Internet is that an audience both capable of and interested in the processing of primary source material already exists. There are currently, however, a limited number of databases comprised of primary source materials available to the network community. Indeed, if visions of the "library without walls" are to be realized, academic libraries must give careful consideration to current database designs.

Academe will move forward in the development of databases containing primary source materials with or without the involvement of libraries. The development of discipline-specific databases will arise from research within scholarly communities. Much as scholars now publish research findings in the traditional print marketplace, databases will be self-published in the network community.

The delivery of primary source material has to be coupled with full-text retrieval in order to provide cost-effective primary source management solutions for libraries. Accessing citations to materials in a networked environment, and then relying upon labor-intensive methods of document delivery is not cost-effective although there will likely be a need for document delivery of items from the historical non-electronic collection for some time to come. There is growing interest in the storage and retrieval of primary source material within the research library community, but to date the majority of research libraries have done relatively little with full-text retrieval systems. Full-text management is a radical departure from the data management with which the library world has become accustomed.

The library standard for machine-readable data, Machine-Readable Cataloging (MARC), was born in a different era of computing and telecommunications. The world of automated text processing has matured considerably since the introduction of the MARC record. Currently, there is a fair amount of debate in the research library community over the need to simplify cataloging procedures and practices. Perhaps there is a need to simplify the standard bibliographic records format for use with more sophisticated computing tools. Proponents of the MARC record will cite the need for quality control of the data in our databases, while the alternate camp advocates the need to control rising costs associated with cataloging of library materials (Graham, September 1990; Knutson 1986; Mandel 1988).

The adoption of full-text retrieval does not require the library community to abandon record structure and quality control of critical database elements. The judicious use of structured text can provide flexibility in performing global updates of authority elements. A common definition of "critical" data elements, however, must first be agreed upon. As primary access points, record elements such as author (and its various permutations) and title warrant a field in a structured record. A strong case can be made that certain highly unique text strings in existing bibliographic records (e.g., ISSN, ISBN, and LCCN) do not require fields of their own in a full-text retrieval system. Optimal methods of handling other elements of the existing MARC record structure, however, are not as clear. There is a definite need for additional research leading to the adoption of record format standards for structured full-text records.

Currently, there is a significant shortage of cost-effective full-text data available from which to build library databases. More data, however, is becoming available everyday, much of it generated within institutions of higher education and on the Internet itself where the vast majority of the nation's research libraries reside. Even more data are being generated in the private sector. Only an insignificant fraction of the data traveling through the traditional print marketplace is not created and processed in machine-readable form. In fact, it is difficult to envision a future in which those data would not be made available to electronic libraries, or some other entity, for use in full-text retrieval systems.

Re-Structuring the Inter-Library Lending Model

The inter-library lending model has evolved in libraries as a natural extension of collection development activities in order to provide an alternative means of providing library users with the materials they need. As recently as ten years ago, the generally accepted principle regarding computerized library networks was that they were a useful tool for collection development and technical processing personnel. The suitability of these networks for processing inter-library lending requests was only beginning to emerge. A vision of a single network shared by the library staff and clientele was not evident.

Katz writes:

> Technology will one day link most of the nation's libraries by online machine-readable data bases and give book selectors at one library immediate information about the selection decisions of librarians in another. This quicker access will make it possible to discover quickly who has what and much easier to decide whether, for example, to buy an extremely expensive, esoteric encyclopedia. The same knowledge may make it easier to persuade users, who now insist the library have all major books and journals, that libraries can share resources without harmful effects on the users' research activities. (1980, 45)

He further notes that the location of a citation for a book in such a network is not the same as having the item in hand. Clearly, he was not thinking of using computer networks as a delivery vehicle for primary source material. In fact, the notion of doing so at the time was considered infeasible by many people. Curiously, Katz's working definition of networks is not computer oriented at all. He states, "computers and communications may be among the tools used for facilitating communications among them [networks]" (1980, 45). Does the research library community still view computer networks in this manner, or has the Internet changed the perspective?

Inter-library loan has already been greatly affected by the introduction of telefacsimile technology. Today, it is common for libraries to send and receive journal articles using telefacsimile. It is also common for faculty to request articles to be "faxed" to their offices rather than to the library due to the inconvenience of retrieving articles in another building on campus. Current inter-library lending policies often prevent this type of interchange as the library staff must receive notification of delivery in order to complete the request process. Extending this scenario, it seems highly likely that faculty are going to want to get networked information delivered directly to their network accounts. What policies will be required to accommodate a wide area document delivery system in the Internet?

Existing library procedures, including inter-library lending, are centered upon a model of ownership and location of physical items. Classification codes are routinely assigned to materials in libraries chiefly as a method of facilitating the storage of the physical item. Books and journals are shelved, microfilm and microfiche are filed in cabinets. In the networked environment, these procedures lose their relevance. The network path statement becomes the defining element for location on the Internet. New sets of policies and procedures need to be developed within libraries to govern how resource sharing will occur in the networked environment. Additionally, new networking tools will be needed to track transactions by users for the library staff, to track transactions for the rights holders to ensure due reimbursement for use of the material, and to perform authentication of both users and documents to ensure the quality of the deliverable product.

CONCLUSION

There are undoubtedly other relevant issues not explored in this paper. Nonetheless, current research library practice faces a great challenge as a result of internetworking. The impact of this challenge, as outlined previously, suggests that massive changes are on the horizon.

The major barriers hindering the development of networked information resources in academic research libraries are not technological in nature. A significant portion of the technical barriers related to full-text storage and retrieval have been conquered with commercially available technology. The challenging frontiers in computer science and networking lie in media file formats, such as graphics, full-motion video, digital sound, and composite document management. The real barriers are managerial or administrative in nature--the adequate training of library staff (and users), the evolution of jobs within the library, and the achievement of inter-organizational cooperation in the adoption of common data formats, technical standards, and resource sharing agreements.

NOTES

1. Paul Evan Peters, Director of the Coalition for Networked Information, has likened the current conditions on the network to the latter three periods of human evolution during the Stone Age–the paleolithic, the mesolithic, and the neolithic periods. Today, in the paleo-electronic era, people are using crude computing and networking tools (e.g., FTP, unix grep, etc.) analogous to stone knives and axes and are engaged in networking activities that are largely predatory in nature. As users enter the meso-electronic era, the networking tools continue to mature and socialization occurs in the community as groups like the Coalition for Networked Information, the Electronic Frontier Foundation, and the Internet Society are formed. The dawn of the neo-electronic era will be upon us when the refined networking tools that lead to humankind's "electronic civilization" appear.

2. For additional information on the TopNode project, contact the author.

3. St. George, Art, and Ronald L. Larsen. *Internet-Accessible Library Catalogs and Databases*. To retrieve this file, send an electronic mail message to the address LISTSERV@UNMVM.BITNET with the only line of the message being GET LIBRARY PACKAGE.

4. Barron, Billy. *UNT's Accessing On-Line Bibliographic Databases*. Use anonymous FTP at ftp.unt.edu to retrieve this file (Directory: LIBRARY File: LIBRARIES.TXT).

5. This topic has been discussed on the Public-Access Computer Systems Forum (PACS-L@UHUPVM1.BITNET).Consult the archives of the PACS-L archives for one of the most complete discussions of this subject. To learn about the LISTSERV system, send an electronic mail message to LISTSERV@UHUP-VM1.BITNET with the only line of the message being INFO REFCARD.

6. The Coalition for Networked Information unveiled a program entitled the Rights for Electronic Access to and Dissemination of Information (READI) in November, 1991. This program is designed to enable a contractual relationship between "subscribers to" and "publishers of" electronic data so the data can be used and distributed in a networked environment. For more information on READI, contact the author.

7. The Info-Mac Digest is published daily as the electronic discussion list INFO-MAC@sumex-aim.stanford.edu,and is archived for anonymous FTP on sumex-aim.stanford.edu. These data are mirrored to several other sites on the network for search and retrieval using other software applications.

BIBLIOGRAPHY

Delzeit, Linda (Director of Education, National Public Telecomputing Network). Electronic mail to author, 4 March 1992.

Gardner, Richard K. *Library Collections: Their Origin, Selection, and Development*. New York: McGraw-Hill, 1981.

Graham, Peter S. "Electronic Information and Research Library Technical Services." *College & Research Libraries* 51, no. 3 (May 1990): 241-250.

Graham, Peter S. "Quality in Cataloging: Making Distinctions." *The Journal of Academic Librarianship* 16, no. 4 (September 1990): 213-218.

Katz, William A. *Collection Development: The Selection of Materials for Libraries*. New York: Holt, Rinehart and Winston, 1980.

Knutson, Gunnar. "Does the Catalog Record Make a Difference? Access Points and Book Use." *College & Research Libraries* 47, no. 5 (September 1986): 460-469.

Larsen, Ronald L. "The Library as a Network-Based Information Server." *EDUCOM Review* 26, no. 3/4 (Fall/Winter 1991): 38-44.

Lottor, Mark K. *Internet Growth (1981-1991)*. Network Information Center, Department of Defense Network, 1992 (available via anonymous FTP at nic.ddn.mil Directory: rfc File: rfc1296.txt).

Lynch, Clifford A. "Linking Library Automation Systems in the Internet: Functional Requirements, Planning, and Policy Issues." *Library Hi-Tech*, no. 28 (1989): 7-18.

Lucier, Richard E. "Knowledge Management: Refining Roles in Scientific Communication." *EDUCOM Review* 25, no. 3 (Fall 1990): 21-27.

Machine-Assisted Reference Section. Reference and Adult Services Division. *Library Resources on the Internet: Strategies for Selection and Use*. Chicago: American Library Association, 1991 (available via anonymous FTP at dlaucop.edu Directory: /pub/internet File: libcat-guide).

Mandel, Carol A. "Trade-offs: Quantifying Quality in Library Technical Services." *The Journal of Academic Librarianship* 14, no. 4 (September 1988): 214-220.

Matheson, N. W., R. E. Lucier, K. A. Butter, and R. E. Reynolds. "The Expanding Role of Libraries in the Academic Health Center." In *Campus Strategies for Libraries and Electronic Information*, edited by Caroline Arms. Bedford, Massachusetts: Digital Press, 1989.

McClure, Charles R., Ann R. Bishop, Philip Doty, and Howard Rosenbaum. *The National Research and Education Network (NREN): Research and Policy Perspectives*. Norwood, NJ: Ablex, 1991.

National Science Foundation, Network Information Center. *NSF91-09.PTRAFFIC*. Merit Computer, Inc., 1991 (available via anonymous FTP at nic.merit.edu Directory: NSFSTATS File: NSF91-09.PTRAFFIC).

Perry, Dennis G., Steven H. Blumenthal, and Robert M. Hinden. "The ARPANET and the DARPA Internet." *Library Hi-Tech* 6, no. 2 (1988): 51-62.

Quarterman, John S. *The Matrix: Computer Networks and Conferencing Systems Worldwide*. Bedford, Massachusetts: Digital Press, 1990.

Rosenthal, Joseph A. "Crumbling Walls: the Impact of the Electronic Age on Libraries and their Clienteles." *Journal of Library Administration* 14, no. 1 (1991): 9-17.

High School Education and the Internet: The Davis Senior High School Experience

Janet Meizel

SUMMARY. This paper outlines the importance of sharing information resources for the intellectual development of high school students. The experiences of Davis Senior High School in connecting to the Internet and other international resources are presented as an illustration of what is possible. The endeavors of the faculty and students are evaluated as an educationally sound extension of the traditional high school curriculum.

Much of our nation's research and communication is now handled by computer-based systems. This has created a myriad of new opportunities for the business and academic worlds. It has also, however, created new challenges for those in the field of education who must provide students with the appropriate knowledge to take advantage of the opportunities. These skills should be taught to high school students before they enter the job market or proceed to university studies. But programs to accomplish this task are expensive, and equipment for students is frequently out of date or simply unavailable due to cost.

Sadly, some teachers and administrators in the field of secondary education consider computer use to be an unnecessary frill. Secondary school libraries have had their funds cut drastically in recent years, and many do not even employ certificated librarians. Furthermore, the publishing date on reference books in many high

Janet Meizel is Computer Science Teacher and Network Manager for the Davis Senior High School, Davis, CA.

© 1992 by The Haworth Press, Inc. All rights reserved.   *127* school libraries would make any researcher cringe. For example, over two thirds of the reference books in Davis High School library, one of the best of its kind in the Sacramento Valley, display copyright dates before 1979. These issues present major concerns if students and teachers are to conduct accurate research. Sharing of resources between academic and school libraries using telecommunications can significantly improve the situation for both teachers and students.

A PARTNERSHIP PROJECT

In an attempt to find solutions to some of the present problems in education, a partnership was formed by the University of California at Davis, Pacific Bell, and Davis Senior High School. Under the auspices of a grant from Pacific Bell and assistance from the Internet Federation, Davis Senior High School (DSHS) and the University of California at Davis (UCD) set up a data link from DSHS to the UCD campus. This data link connected DSHS's computer lab to UCD's computer network and has, for over a year, provided access to a wide variety of data available through UCD's Internet connection. This connection has allowed the high school to expand its computer studies curriculum, thus opening new horizons for students interested in computer applications and research. It also affords opportunities for innovative teaching and work methods for students and faculty in the other departments at DSHS.

The University of California at Davis is heavily involved in computer network research and actively participates in international network standards committees. Computer networks are becoming an increasingly important utility, particularly in the academic and research communities. UCD is currently connected to all three of the major international networks that are used for educational and research information exchange (Internet, BITNET, and USENET),[1] plus BARRNet (Bay Area Regional Research Network) and NSF-Net (National Science Foundation Network). By virtue of these UCD connections, DSHS has access to UCD campus resources, as well as statewide, regional, national, and international resources.

Davis Senior High School is the largest campus in the Davis

Joint Unified School District with an enrollment of approximately 1,200 students. As a comprehensive high school, it has strong community support. At the time of this writing the district was working on the third in a series of bond issues to raise money for needed repairs, and an override tax to support classroom education has been passed twice in the last ten years. The district otherwise has limited resources. One of the stated purposes of this project is to determine whether it is worthwhile to attempt this type of connection for a secondary school and to develop a prototype low-cost system to support the effort.

A 56 Kilobit per second (Kbps) Advanced Digital Network (ADN) circuit is the data link from DSHS directly to the UCD campus. This service provides high quality digital transmission as well as variable data speeds, error detection, and potential for expansion. Within the high school, cables have been laid from the present 25-computer network and its server to the library. Additionally, cables have been run to classrooms in anticipation of computers in these areas. Apple Computer, Inc. has provided the high school with a network server (Macintosh IICX) and additional hardware and software to support the local area network. They have also provided computers for additional classroom stations, two CD-ROM drives, and a flatbed scanner.

Joan Gargano, of the UCD Computer Services Department, has provided programs for the Macintosh computers which use a graphical-user-interface and make telecommunications easy for the user. Early versions of the software were not as transparent as more recent iterations, thus discouraging some of the teachers. Present programs require only the knowledge to boot the machine and use pull-down menus.

GETTING STARTED

The first groups of teachers (about 50 out of 70 teachers) and students (approximately 300) have been trained to use the network, and their reaction has been favorable. All users of our Internet connection must understand the rules and responsibilities of network use, both at the local level and for our university connection.

Each user is required to read the UCD manual of computer etiquette and sign a document which states that they agree to these requirements and the additional ones which DSHS has imposed. The teachers and students understand that infractions will result in revocation of the privilege of network use.

NETWORK RESOURCES

Three recent additions to the networks illustrate the nature of resources available to participants who are connected. Although still in beginning stages, these offerings are providing significant opportunities for secondary students.

Cleveland Free-Net

The most established is Cleveland Free-Net.[2] During the past winter, it began the Academy One project which is designed for teachers and students. Academy One provides students with many research and correspondence opportunities, as well as providing medical information specifically designed for school personnel. For example, information is offered on how a particular condition or medication may affect a student in a classroom situation.

Some of the projects currently listed under Academy One are Historical Documents, Congressional Memory Project, Hermes, and the Electronic Bookshelf and Reference Desk. There are also many other areas within Cleveland Free-Net of benefit to students, beyond those intended specifically for academic use, including Science and Technology and even the USA Today headline news.

The Historical Documents section contains pre-Constitution documents; the Constitution and documents of its era; and post-Constitution documents, poetry, sayings, and songs. The Congressional Memory Project contains bills as they are passed each week, along with the specific House/Senate member voting records. There is also a section which contains the addresses of Congresspersons, along with the suggestion that letter writers request that representatives make themselves available by electronic mail (e-mail)!

Hermes is the means of electronically distributing the decisions of the Supreme Court. Supreme Court information and the Congressional Memory Project come to the Cleveland Free-Net via the National Public Telecomputing Network.[3] Files can be downloaded to a computer for searching or annotation with a word processor, if needed.

Other sections of this bulletin board are the Electronic bookshelf, which contains complete texts of the Bible (King James version), The Book of Mormon, and the Koran. The somewhat limited selection is due to copyright considerations, although the selection is increasing over time. The World Fact Book contains statistics on the nations of the world, the oceans, and the planet. In the Spanish II classes, DSHS students have been using a CD-ROM version of the World Fact Book for reports on Spanish-speaking countries. Using a major external database, however, will have the advantages of frequent updates which cannot be afforded locally, and support for more than one user at a time.

The Reference Desk, another part of the Electronic Bookshelf, is a bulletin board for posting questions and answers of the type usually asked of a reference librarian. There are also areas with information about international organizations, the United Nations, weights and measures, definitions, abbreviations, and GAO reports.

Students may use Cleveland Free-Net as visitors, but some students have found it to be so valuable that they have applied for individual accounts. Having a personal account allows them to enter chat areas and send e-mail.

TRIE

A second resource for California teachers is the TRIE[4] network, run by the California Technology Project. Although this resource is in its infancy, it contains some useful databases such as Cable News Network guides, curriculum guides, video and software evaluations, and bulletin boards and conference opportunities. It is also starting a project called "What is Japan?" where users will be able to ask questions about Japan which will be answered by Japanese users.

National Energy Research Supercomputer Center

A third very new resource is provided by the Department of Energy National Energy Research Supercomputer Center (NERSC) at the Lawrence Livermore National Laboratory. This project will allow schools with trained personnel to use a Cray supercomputer to create climate simulations and ray-traced, three-dimensional movies. These programs can be useful in physical and biological sciences, as well as for mathematical modeling and art and computer science classes. They will also maintain a bulletin board targeted toward the educational user. Teachers will be able to prepare movies to use as illustrations in the classroom, and students can use the computer as a creative tool while practicing the skills and exercising knowledge gained from the classroom.

THE INTERNET

The Internet provides a great deal of information for all users. Various computers available via the Internet hold documents that can be downloaded. For example, the Association of Research Libraries publishes a directory of electronic journals, newsletters and digests, including items of interest to social sciences and humanities scholars. Project Gutenberg and the Cleveland Free-Net Academy One project provide full-text files of such things as Lewis Carroll's work. Merit, one of the organizations involved in managing the National Science Foundation Network (NSFNet), made various iterations of the House of Representatives version of the High Performance Computing Act available as it was being considered by Congress. Equal Access to Software for Instruction (EASI) recently published the sections of the Americans with Disabilities Act and other related documents. All of these files could be easily used by teachers and students.

The Internet and other networks provide access to discussion groups and archives of material for specific interest groups, covering virtually every field of academic and ancillary interest from archaeology to biomedical hypermedia instructional design. These groups (lists) hail from all over the world. For example, one list on artificial intelligence is run from Monterrey, Mexico. Another is run from Japan. Individuals may subscribe to these lists to receive regular communications or may search the archives of previous discussions as desired. The KIDSNET mailing list, for example, is open to anyone with an interest in K-12 education. Subscribers receive daily communications with information useful for either the classroom or the school environment.

STUDENT APPLICATIONS

Students are constant users of the computers on both the local school network and the Internet. Journalism students have used Internet resources for their newspaper articles. Students at all skill levels use the word-processing facilities for writing essays and reports. Several students are using computer graphics programs for art classes and for personal creative activities. Many download public domain graphics for use in reports and other projects. The option of creating three-dimensional ray-traced moving graphics via the Cray computer connection will probably greatly increase use of graphic capabilities.

There is a continuous flow of students using the USENET News-groups, both for official schoolwork and to follow personal interests. The most popular newsgroups are those which discuss the Space Shuttle (physics students), international relations (international relations and history students), various computer languages (computer science students), and music and ethnic groups. Other students have joined the "talk groups" on UCD's network and have read and responded to articles on topics ranging from aeronautics and physics to discussions of the Middle East, "C" language for the computer, music, and recent political events.

Students who explore the Internet have found several "chat" boards on which they can have real-time conversations with college students and others in the academic world. Students gain valuable information from some of these chats. This aspect of network use excites the curiosity of many, while providing them with writing skills practice in a non-threatening arena.

One of the chief attractions of this type of communication is that the students are seen as equal participants in the communication process, rather than "kids playing with the computers." Their comments must be carefully thought out and are given consideration equal to that given to messages from the other members of the discussion. This promotes a form of "electronic democracy," one of the themes in which Pacific Bell has shown strong interest.

Several students, who have strong ties to high school graduates now attending college, have used the e-mail capability to correspond with and receive encouragement from these friends. Students at other universities with access to the Internet have volunteered to discuss their college programs with DSHS students and have offered advice on college admissions and programs. Many students have used the California State University at Sacramento bulletin board to help them decide which California State University they might attend and to look up information on majors, housing, costs, etc. A computer has been placed in the Career and Scholarship Center at DSHS so that students have greater access to the network for college planning purposes. Several other universities also maintain open bulletin boards which have postings of course catalogues, major requirements, fees, etc.

CLASSROOM APPLICATIONS

Along with the students, many of the teachers are enthusiastic about use of the network, most notably those in the foreign language, English, and mathematics departments. A significant number of students and teachers are using MELVYL (the University of California online library catalogue) for library research assistance. MELVYL not only contains the University of California library catalogues but has online links to many other university libraries. The DSHS Librarian, Sharon Hallberg, now includes use of MELVYL in the classes she teaches for the English Department. These sessions are part of the standard English curriculum and introduce the students to library resources. Students are trained to widen or narrow their searches using the standard boolean operators "and" and "or." They also explore the MELVYL system during training to discover its capabilities and limitations. Once students are trained, they can use MELVYL's search capabilities in several ways.

They can do a standard search for books on a given topic or by a particular author. This is the first type of search they are taught and is immediately useful to computer students for an assignment. They must look up books by authors of their own surname. While this provokes much laughter and conversation, it gives them an idea of the variety of works available.

The second type of search students learn is the browse option. This is very popular among students who have been assigned to write a paper on one aspect of a broad topic. The teacher of the Advanced Placement[5] music course, for example, annually assigns a fifty-minute presentation and accompanying paper on a topic related to music history. Music students this year used MELVYL's browse search, which yielded many subtopics, some of which contained even more specific subgroups. After looking at the array of topics, students were able to ascertain their own interests and bring up an instant bibliography of books available at the nearby U.C. library. Not only did MELVYL help the students create their final projects, but it also played a significant role in finding a suitable subject. The U.C. library has also allowed teachers at the High School to apply for checkout privileges at this facility, a concession which makes access to MELVYL even more useful.

Several classes have used the information stored on CD-ROM databases for classroom reports. Because of the ease of use (and perhaps the novelty), students constantly browse through our CD-ROM library (two history databases, a database with information on various countries, a science database, a public domain software collection, and several discs containing programming information). During the year, the librarian purchased another CD-ROM system so that users could research periodical abstracts. Periodical abstracts are not presently an option on any of the databases which DSHS can reach via the Internet. The combination of internal and external resources provides a broad range of research material for students and teachers.

TEACHER APPLICATIONS

An additional benefit of network access is the increase in the general use of computers by teachers. Teachers already use the computers for planning, word-processing and other classroom tasks. Network access permits additional research (MELVYL, bulletin boards, and newsgroups), participation in discussions, and use of e-mail systems. Teachers can communicate with other teachers and authorities in specialized fields and use external databases as sources of new information for classroom support. Mentorships have been arranged using e-mail and chat capabilities, so that individual students can receive appropriate assistance. One teacher, Cliff Simes, found an additional bulletin board to use–one devoted to teachers in Vocational Education (CAVIX). Access will become easier for him, and for all teachers, when computers are placed in all classrooms and connected to the network. He also plans to encourage his students to use the network to keep abreast of current world events for history courses.

Teachers are able to communicate with professional organizations over the Internet, including the Modern Language Association, American Association of Teachers of Spanish and Portuguese, Association of Teachers of French, American Association of Teachers of German, American Association of Teachers of Mathematics, etc. They can also download public domain software from software collections to support instruction and aid in classroom management. We have discovered that it is more efficient for advanced students to do the downloading and decompression of software for the teachers, unless the teachers are particularly interested in the process.

Teachers and students in the Foreign Language Department use the network for e-mail to other classes and immediate classroom connections to information sources that will be used in discussions and projects (backup statistics, news items, etc.). They will also use network resources to support individual or small-group cooperative work in classroom settings. The focus for the coming year will be integration of the network into the curricula followed at the school site. As users are becoming more familiar with the possibilities offered by the network, they more clearly see its relevance to their particular subjects and how use of the resources on the Internet can benefit their particular classes. A committee has been formed with representatives from each department. They will plan and provide support for the integration of network use into the curriculum.

Classroom lesson plans and materials must be developed to cover the basic elements of the curricula so that beginning teacher/network users will be secure enough in their plans to participate. These plans can easily be distributed via e-mail to other schools who want to participate in joint projects.

PROBLEMS ENCOUNTERED

When the project began, many observers were concerned about potential problems. They were afraid that high school students might cause damage to the UCD network or to the Internet itself. Some observers said that the process of using the network would be too difficult for students of that age. Once the programs providing access to various aspects of the Internet were tested, and user-friendly versions installed, access became easy enough for even the least computer-sophisticated teacher or student to use.

Throughput and activities originating from high school accounts are monitored by both the DSHS Network Manager and the UCD Network Manager. This oversight is the network manager's prerogative and responsibility on all networks. Both the high school staff and students have been made aware of the situation. Staff at the UCD library have provided us with guides to MELVYL and the UC library system. Everyone at the school who has access to the network has read the documents and promised to follow the UC and DSHS guidelines. They know that even with the grant and the tremendous amount of help we are receiving, responsibility for the success of this project rests with the students and faculty at the school. The students have their own accounts, providing them with a sense of ownership, resulting in even fewer problems than we anticipated.

The major problems we have faced have not been of student origin. Some of them are caused by the overabundance of materials. There is so much information available, it is sometimes difficult to narrow a search to include only what is necessary. The students love to explore the Internet and are often sidetracked by what they find. It is rather like reading the entire encyclopedia as you find interesting articles. One student, writing a paper on the subject of "hackers," found so much information that he had to ask the teacher for a deadline extension so that he could cull the information he needed. Other students were fascinated by the files which had been compiled about "cold fusion" and spent hours perusing the debate. The Internet is so large that a definitive "Yellow Pages" type of guidebook has not been constructed. Creating such a directory is a current project of the Internet Federation, so future use will be easier. So much information is constantly being recorded, however, that maintaining a directory could be a never-ending task.

Another problem is one of lack of time and money. Unlike the students, many teachers feel that they do not have the time to explore. Any new technique to which they will subscribe must make teaching and student learning easier, not just add another task to their day. The computer must be available when they need it and where they need it. They want exact directions and specific information. They must have compelling reasons to use telecomputing.

Although the Science Department has shown little interest in use of the network (only biological sciences teachers want to use the resource), the Mathematics Department has asked for an in-service training session to learn how to use the programs to access the Cray. One mathematics class has already begun work in the computer laboratory. Previously, the department had been somewhat reticent about network use, but, now that the teachers have an immediate reason to use it, they are eager. A reason to use it and ease of access to outside resources will most certainly be the key to use by the rest of the teachers.

During this project the school district has been forced to cut its budget. To support the Internet-use project, a raffle was held to raise money. These funds plus local contributions will provide monies for payment of the fee for the leased 56 Kbps line for another year and possible expansion of our local area network to more classrooms. The $1200 fee for the 56 Kbps line may seem extravagant for a high school at first glance, but this type of Internet connection allows many people to use the network simultaneously with no time-based use charges. An entire class can get hands-on experience with the teacher guiding them from a central station. Each student can then participate in an individual project at his or her own pace, thus individualizing the curriculum being taught and encouraging a much higher level of participation and success.

PROJECT EVALUATION

Increasing participation and success for students has been one of the major advantages of the Internet connection. The project has been beneficial to students at all levels of academic and technical achievement. It also appears to be equally popular with students of both sexes and all ethnic groups. This phenomenon runs contrary to representation in traditional programming and advanced applications classes, where male students still outnumber the females despite several years of recruitment. During the first year of this project, two migrant students were placed in an Advanced Applications course. They learned the usual curriculum, plus use of the Internet, and participated in USENET Newsgroups and e-mail consistently. At the end of the year, when students signed up for the next year's courses, most of the school's migrant population registered for the class. This notable change is most encouraging. One of the prevailing issues of the future will be the dichotomy between the technologically and informationally literate and those who are unprepared for the information age.

Although at the time of this writing the project is still in its "working stage," it is evident that the Internet connection is a catalyst for changes in the classroom and for individual student participation in the learning process. Final statistics have not been compiled, but there has been a noticeable shift in attitude about computer use among both students and the majority of the faculty. Results of the beginning questionnaire showed that only 2 out of 138 students had non-computer-science teachers who assigned computer-assisted tasks to their students. At the end of the first full year of network use, 64% had two or more teachers who did so.

Is it appropriate that high schools be connected to the Internet? The experience of the Davis Senior High School suggests a resounding "Yes." Few innovations have the potential importance in the intellectual and vocational development of students as learning to use the facilities provided by the Internet connection. And few shared resources have the breadth and depth of the Internet. It is imperative, however, that educators view such an issue not as a "frill" or as a resource for the privileged few, but as instrumental in the establishment of an educated populace, a necessary component to cope with the challenges of the information age.

NOTES

1. Internet is an international network of networks, including institutions of higher learning, government agencies, research organizations, and commercial establishments. These networks support electronic mail, file transfer, and remote logon services.

BITNET, Because It's Time NETwork, links more than 2,300 hosts in 32 countries. This network supports electronic mail and file transfer primarily for the academic community.

USENET, one of the largest networks with over 9,700 hosts, is a collection of sites and individuals that cooperatively build electronic discussion groups, and information repositories.

2. Cleveland Free-Net, located at Case Western Reserve University in Cleveland, Ohio, is a publicly-accessible database and bulletin board service providing data and access to the Internet at no charge.

3. The National Public Telecomputing Network is a not-for-profit corporation that promotes community-based computer networks in cities around the U.S. It was formed after the phenomenal success of Cleveland Free-Net.

4. TRIE is a network of the California Technology Project, in conjunction with the California State Department of Education. It provides information resources and access to the Internet for schools in California that have telecommunications capabilities. It is centered at the California State University system.

5. An Advanced Placement course offers high school students the opportunity to qualify for college credit at many universities.

Technology-Driven Resource Sharing:
A View of the Future

James E. Rush

SUMMARY. Resource sharing, the use, in common, by two or more libraries of personnel, equipment, facilities, knowledge, expertise, and information resources, is no longer an option; it is the very essence of service to their clientele. This article presents resource sharing in a new light wherein real cooperation, automation, and data communication are the keys to effective and efficient resource sharing. New pricing and charging strategies and improvements in resource sharing through regional networks are also discussed.

INTRODUCTION

Resource sharing is most often discussed in the context of bibliographic materials and is achieved through the process of interlibrary loan–an extension of circulation, the primary resource sharing function. Although resource sharing in this traditional conception is important today, it cannot continue to be justified, much less supported, as an important means of sharing resources because: (1) It is labor intensive and therefore quite costly (and such costs will only increase); (2) it causes resources to be out of the reach of everyone but the client to whom they have been lent (in fact, they are out of the reach of everyone during transit); (3) it involves distribution costs (i.e., packaging, shipping, receiving, record-keeping) that are significant and increasing; and (4) it is not timely, frequently taking a week or two to get materials into the hands of

James E. Rush is Executive Director of PALINET. The views expressed herein are those of the author and do not necessarily reflect those of PALINET.

© 1992 by The Haworth Press, Inc. All rights reserved.

141

a client. Traditional resource sharing also reflects too limited a view of what resource sharing should encompass.

SCOPE OF RESOURCE SHARING

Through an expanded vision of resource sharing, one can envision the sharing of knowledge and expertise among libraries. To be fully realized, such efforts must involve combining staff, centralizing cataloging at the regional or national level, integrating collection development, and sharing equipment (especially expensive equipment) and facilities.

Prime candidates for sharing are ones that require considerable capital outlay and significant recurring operating costs (e.g., integrated library systems). Resource sharing, however, can and must extend to include the sharing of staff resources, particularly specialized ones, such as system operators, catalogers, acquisitions librarians, and serials management personnel. Resource sharing should also include the sharing of facilities, such as processing areas, storage facilities, bookmobiles, and meeting space.

In short, resource sharing should encompass information, personnel, equipment, facilities, and expertise. Part of this sharing of resources can be accomplished without automation support. For resource sharing to be truly effective and efficient, however, automation and data communication are essential. Nevertheless, considerable improvement in resource sharing, and thus in the cost of operation of libraries, can be achieved through stronger cooperation among libraries.

The remainder of this paper details the argument that resource sharing in this technological age must be based on data communication networks (i.e., the merger of traditional library automation systems and data communications), rather than on hard-copy materials and manual transmission. No other practical way exists to provide the services clients need and deserve. It is assumed that such services are delivered through data communication networks provided by libraries.

RESOURCE SHARING VIA CIRCULATION

Circulation is the basic method of sharing bibliographic resources of the library with clients. In the manner in which circulation has been, and continues to be, performed, even with automation support, bibliographic resources are shared with a single client at a time. As a consequence, simultaneous access to a given item can be provided only by acquiring and housing multiple copies, or through interlibrary loan (if, in fact, local interlibrary agreements permit borrowing an owned item). The process is labor intensive and is very costly for libraries. It also entails an ownership issue that complicates matters unnecessarily and restricts client access to resources.

A method, independent of real or expected demand, geographical location of material or client, and medium of expression (e.g., paper, plastic, film, magnetic disk, or tape), is needed for sharing resources. In short, information resources must be represented in machine-readable form and accessible via data communication networks. Information resources so represented can be made available to everyone who wants access to them, either simultaneously or sequentially, without regard to the geographical location of the person or the information resource.

Moreover, information resources represented in machine-readable form can be delivered to the client in the format most suitable to the client (e.g., audio, textual, graphical, large print, or any combination of these). In essence, machine-readable information resources can be delivered to the client when, where, and in the amount needed, irrespective of any access to or use of the same resource by any other person.

A NEW PUBLISHING MODEL

In order to achieve this objective, a fundamental change in the process of publication must occur. Articles, chapters, books, manuscripts of speeches, music scores, sound recordings, maps, and other forms of material are increasingly being prepared in machine-readable form. The first installation of such materials on a data communication network designed specifically for access by the public will constitute "publication" in the same sense in which these materials become "published" when committed to paper and reproduced for distribution under the current model. Such installation must become the first and principal means of distribution.

This new method of publication will reduce the cost of publication by eliminating the guess-work in determining the number of copies to produce. To be sure, there will be some initial cost of this method of publication, since there may still be editorial work, design, and layout, at least where quality and peer review are deemed important to the publication. There may also be a charge for installing (i.e., publishing) an item on a data communication network. Reproduction and distribution costs, however, will no longer be up-front costs. Instead, they will be associated with the delivery of the item, or parts of it, to the requesting client.

While simply making these publications available on a data communication network accords them copyright protection, the data communication networks will need to be able to register each publication with the appropriate copyright agency to account for all uses of the publication, to charge appropriately for such use, and to account for publisher fees, author royalties, system use fees, telecommunication costs, and so on.

EXPECTED OUTCOMES

There are several important outcomes of the widespread availability of machine-readable information resources. First, any item can be delivered to any person at any time regardless of the location of either the person or the item. Second, an item, or any part thereof, can be presented to the client in a variety of forms, including hard-copy, machine-readable, graphic, audio (e.g., audio output for the vision impaired), tactile, etc.

For entire books, articles, sound recordings, music scores, maps, and other forms of material, on-demand publishing for use in hand-held or lap-top readers designed for single or multi-media presentation can be achieved. Although some would argue that the printed book will never cease to exist (and it may not), the number of books produced in their present form will decline dramatically as personal readers are developed and become popular.

Given the fact that a large quantity of hard-copy material exists, the data communication networks on which new items are published must also be capable of identifying the existence and availability of traditionally published materials regardless of their physical location. Moreover, it makes sense to convert such materials to machine-readable form based on demand. And finally, the cost per unit of service of such highly enhanced library services should be less than for traditionally published materials.

RESOURCE SHARING VIA INTERLIBRARY LOAN

Interlibrary loan (ILL) will be meaningless as a method of sharing resources when materials are represented in machine-readable form. ILL, however, may be used for existing hard-copy materials. In the interest of making these materials more widely available, it would be far better if any such material that was requested by a client were immediately converted to machine-readable form and stored on a data communication network. Interlibrary loan, as the process is known, cannot be supported in the future because of its cost and the inherent limits on access to materials that it imposes.

OTHER SHARED PROCESSING

Circulation and interlibrary loan, two traditional processes libraries routinely perform, will be greatly altered, or entirely eliminated, as information resources are published in machine-readable form. All other library processes will also be greatly altered in scope and character as a consequence of the availability of information resources via data communication networks.

Cataloging

Individual libraries cannot afford to catalog materials as they have in the past. The process is too costly, and there is no logical justification for the process, even if it were not so costly. It simply makes no economic or intellectual sense to catalog the same work hundreds or thousands of times. Once will do! The repetitive cataloging presently performed does not even provide good access to the materials the process is intended to describe and categorize.

The cataloging process must be centralized so that a published item is cataloged once and only once (i.e., no local practice allowed). Such cataloging should be triggered by the publishing of an item on a data communication network, and the process should concentrate on quality, consistency, and deep subject indexing at least to the section level (or equivalent subdivision) of the publication. Since the entire publication will be accessible online, full-text retrieval should be linked to the cataloging information.

Cataloging is a labor-intensive process; such labor must be truly productive. Alternatively, since the entire content of each publication will be available online, one might argue that cataloging could be foregone without loss of access. Cataloging, however, performed centrally and done well can provide excellent online retrieval. Furthermore, a variety of automated tools that are presently unavailable could be developed to assist the process (e.g., good syndetic devices for subject indexing, use of tables of contents and indexes as part of the catalog record, spelling checkers, authoritative lists of terms, etc.).

If each published item were given twice the attention now paid to the item by a single library, far superior access could be provided at a small fraction of the cost of cataloging today. Cataloging would become a very specialized endeavor with only the brightest and best individuals employed for the work and with each library sharing the results of their work.

Acquisitions

Since everything published will be available via data communication networks, there will no longer be any need for the acquisition function. Every library, by definition, will acquire everything published. There will be no need for ever-increasing amounts of physical storage space, so a library can devote resources to reader space, general public spaces, and to areas for staff support of

clients. The "edifice complex" will be eradicated. The most important issue that must be solved is how to pay for access to an unlimited collection of published materials.

Serials Control

Because every form of material will be published by making it available on a data communication network shared by two or more libraries, there will be no need for local serials control. Instead, a centralized bibliographic control function is needed that works with publishers and authors to insure consistent chronology and enumeration, that deals with notification of availability of given issues (and parts thereof), and that provides centralized deep indexing in areas not presently handled well by abstracting and indexing services.

Data communication networks will automatically handle charges for copying all or parts of a work (serial or otherwise), regardless of the means of copying. In addition, royalties and other costs associated with use of published materials will be accounted for by the data communication networks.

Management

Shared management of libraries is a possibility, although the need is not so strong as is the need for sharing in other areas. Better, stronger management in each individual library is really needed. Management must take the initiative to effect the changes that will bring the future envisioned in this article, or any other shared future, into reality. Lacking such visionary management, the institutions now known as libraries will stagnate and die, while other organizations take control of information access and delivery.

SHARED PERSONNEL AND EXPERTISE

There are a number of functional areas within libraries wherein the sharing of personnel and expertise can improve service and reduce costs. This aspect of resource sharing complements that of shared processes.

Public Service Orientation

First, it is important to understand that the changes in processing described previously must reduce the need for technical services librarians and associated staff, and increase the need for public services personnel. Most libraries are not oriented to public service, despite their claims to the contrary. Commitment to public service can be measured in terms of the number of staff devoted to this function, the attitudes toward the public expressed directly and indirectly by these staff, and the nature and extent of services offered to all clients. Ultimately, the clients will measure the effectiveness of a particular library's commitment to service.

Reference Services

Reference services is one area that can be improved substantially through sharing of personnel and expertise. These units will continue to be important to a large percentage of the population for a long time to come. Libraries in a given community can pool reference staff, centralize telephone reference, and build an understanding of the strengths of each reference librarian. In this way, reference questions can be handled expeditiously, effectively, and efficiently at lower cost than any individual library can achieve.

The goal of reference services should be to reach as many people as possible, providing them with useful information at the lowest cost possible. This goal cannot be met if every library persists in operating a reference service independently.

Training and Continuing Education for Clients

Since availability of and access to information resources will be common to all libraries, it will be possible to improve and strengthen the training and continuing education programs of libraries correspondingly. Here, too, shared effort and shared expertise can be implemented, since staff devoted to training and continuing education for clients will not be needed by each library separately.

For example, if six libraries within a community (e.g., one public library with two branches, one academic library, two school libraries, and two special libraries) pooled their training and continuing education personnel and expertise, two full-time staff could perform all necessary training and continuing education, whereas each individual organization might need one-half to one full-time equivalent to do a less effective job.

Client Special Services

Certain services that require specialized equipment, materials, or staff expertise (e.g., service to the blind and physically handicapped, service to shut-ins, children's and youth's services, and special services to business and industry) can be provided effectively and more efficiently if libraries share the necessary resources. Automation support for services to the blind and physically handicapped, staff with expertise in children's services, and similar resources can be shared so that better overall service is provided at lower cost than individual libraries can achieve.

SHARED FACILITIES

Although it is more difficult to share physical facilities because of logistical problems, there are nevertheless real savings to be achieved if certain kinds of facilities are shared.

Reduced Space Needs

Where geographic location does not preclude it, the sharing of space among two or more libraries is possible. Even when such sharing is not possible, the sharing of processing and personnel makes possible a reduction in the space needed in each individual library. Thus, the opportunity presents itself to use the space for other purposes (e.g., meeting rooms, reader space). As more publications appear in machine-readable form, space needed to house them decreases rapidly–the contents of one CD-ROM disk are equivalent to about 30 linear feet of shelf space. As processes such as cataloging are centralized, the space previously needed for such work can be freed for more productive uses. In short, effective sharing of resources will all but eliminate the drive of librarians to build more space.

Shared Use of Computer Facilities

Computer facilities include rooms with a specialized electrical supply and possibly raised flooring; heating, ventilating and air conditioning (HVAC); telecommunication facilities; and support space, equipment, and personnel. Since computer facilities represent significant capital and operating expenditures for an individual library, they are excellent candidates for sharing. For example, a computer facility capable of supporting computer operations for three or four libraries would cost perhaps 10% to 15% more than a facility supporting just one. Furthermore, it may also provide better operating conditions and fail-safe capabilities. Even if extended hours of coverage by operations personnel were required, a facility shared by four libraries could afford around the clock coverage whereas an individual institution probably could not.

Shared Integrated Library Systems

In addition to shared computer facilities, libraries could achieve significant economic and service gains by sharing integrated systems (i.e., local systems). A major hurdle to overcome is achieving agreement among two or more institutions on the system of choice. Cost savings that derive from shared systems include savings in hardware and software costs, installation costs, operating costs (including maintenance), and upgrade costs.

To be sure, an integrated system shared by two libraries will not reduce capital expenditures by half. Some system vendors employ pricing schemes that obviate such large savings. Nevertheless, the capital outlay would be less than double that of each of two libraries procuring systems separately. In addition, the savings in operating costs will be much closer to 50% of these costs if borne individually. When these savings are added to the savings achieved through shared computer facilities, the benefits of shared systems are unassailable.

PAYING FOR SERVICES

The opportunities for and benefits of resource sharing outlined here can only be attained through strong, innovative management, through better financial strategies, and through effective financial management systems. For individual libraries to abandon local cataloging, for example, in favor of a centralized service, a significant change in philosophy of operation must occur. For libraries to provide significantly improved services, innovative methods of financing library operations are needed.

Libraries continue to experience difficulties in financing operations and providing clients with services when and where needed. To be sure, some of this difficulty is a consequence of pricing strategies employed by publishers, whether the material is published in machine-readable form or not. Nevertheless, the traditional methods of financing library operations have proved woefully inadequate. Yet, few have been bold enough to address the problem in a realistic fashion. The notion that libraries are, or ought to be, free is just a myth.

The Pricing Dilemma

One of the fundamental characteristics of publishing via a tangible medium of expression is that of the unit with which a price is associated: the physical piece. Whether the unit is a journal article, a journal subscription, a book, a sound recording, a map, or other object, the object carries a unit price. Pricing associated with definable physical pieces, from books to airplanes, is well understood. Although the price associated with a physical object need bear no clear relation to the cost of production of the object, people generally accept the object's price as the fair value of the object.

In contrast, publication in machine-readable form forces one to consider significantly different pricing mechanisms, since one can no longer associate a unit price with any tangible medium of expression. A person may search a database and view responses on a video display device without ever committing the retrieved data to some tangible medium. Nevertheless, there is the presumption that the user gains something from such access. Also, significant cost is associated with the provision of such access. Someone must bear this cost. The questions are: Who pays? and How does one pay? Transaction pricing can result in unpredictable revenue streams for authors, publishers, and distributors of information resources, and in unpredictable expenditures for users and libraries.

Producers of electronic publications certainly have a problem with pricing, since many cannot resolve the apparent conflict between multiple copy pricing and network access pricing–a conflict that derives from the notion of a definable physical object. This problem is most evident with CD-ROM databases. Electronic publishers have seized on the notion that the unit to be priced is the entire publication cast in a tangible medium of expression–CD-ROM. The correct unit to be priced, however, is not the publication, but each individual element of the publication that may be retrieved by a given individual.

Nevertheless, electronic publishers are reluctant to price their products in this way because of difficulties in collecting, and because revenues would be collected after use, rather than in advance, as at present. Because of current pricing practices of electronic publishers, expectations for sales of many machine-readable publications are not high. The number of persons or organizations that can, or will, pay from $500 to $5,000 per year for a subscription or license to a single publication is clearly limited. This limitation is particularly evident when one also considers the restricted subject matter of many of these publications.

The pricing problem is illustrated, in part, by a given amount of data cast in different tangible media of expression: from paper to CD-ROM. The cost of producing the data probably varies little with the medium of expression, but the cost of reproduction and distribution varies considerably by medium. Thus, although a publication on CD-ROM costs less to reproduce and distribute than the equivalent amount of data cast as print on paper, in changing media one has lost the smaller units with which prices may be associated in the print product.

This problem is somewhat analogous to the difference between being able to buy single issues of a periodical instead of a multiple-issue subscription. The shift to data distribution via data communication networks (i.e., electronic publishing) must be accompanied by a change in pricing that permits large numbers of users to buy access to small pieces of a publication, instead of a small number of customers buying access to the publication as a whole.

The challenge is to find the correct pricing of data that is accessed through data communication networks, whether such access occurs locally or remotely. Ideally, every piece of data accessed by an individual or enterprise should carry a price tag. OCLC, for example, recently introduced FirstSearch, an online reference service designed to support pricing based on use of the "find" command (i.e., transaction pricing, not physical unit pricing). This approach to pricing obviates the need for pricing according to quantities of data accessed and eliminates the problem of value that pricing based on articles, chapters, abstracts, or other such units of data would imply. Moreover, OCLC's pricing scheme supports advance payment (with suitable refunds for unused "finds"), akin to subscription pricing now prevalent. This pricing scheme also permits wholesale and retail sales of searches, thus permitting libraries to profit from retailing the service.

The way out of the dilemma posed at the beginning of this section, namely the conflict between freedom of access and the fiscal expectations of authors, publishers, and distributors, cannot be achieved by libraries or producers alone. There must be some form of partnership or alliance that will benefit society as a whole as well as those in the information industry. Publisher pricing today is generally skewed because it is based on the wrong sales unit. By pricing large chunks of data as a unit, expectations for sales are predictably low and unit prices are high. Publishers must come to grips with what is actually being sold. Data are sold, not entire publications. This means that the potential for sales of small units contained within a publication should be much greater and that total revenues should be much greater than revenues derived from publications sold, leased, or licensed as a whole.

By pricing on the basis of units of data actually accessed, rather than on entire publications, the issue of single-user versus network pricing disappears. Moreover, such a pricing scheme has the potential for getting data into the hands and minds of a much larger portion of the populace than do present schemes. The model OCLC has introduced points in the right direction, if it is not ultimately the best scheme.

Library Charging Options

If publishers and/or distributors are to be successful in basing their pricing on units such as individual searches, or similar small units, libraries must foster this pricing by requiring users to pay a fee for access to the data. Libraries will be able to offer more data, and a greater variety of data, by recovering operating costs through fees for use of the data provided. Such fees need not prevent anyone from gaining access to needed or desired data or services.

A library typically issues each client an identification card which is, or can be, renewed annually or more frequently. This card entitles the carrier to specified library services. An ID card could be used as a debit card as well. The value of the debit card at issuance (i.e., the amount of access it will buy) would depend on a predetermined base value, an industry standard uniform pricing mechanism, and client-added value.

Every person or enterprise that meets the library's criteria for client status would be granted a certain number of dollars worth of access without having to pay the library any out-of-pocket money. The dollars granted, from zero to a library-defined upper limit, would depend upon client type and status and library type and funding. Client types, on the one hand, might include pre-schooler, youth, adult, business person, professional, senior, shut-in, governmental agency, law firm, or any other necessary category. Client status, on the other hand, could identify users as student, employed, unemployed, retired, convalescent, for-profit, or non-profit. Libraries vary by type (e.g., public, special, school, academic, integrated), and by level of general fiscal support from a parent organization or agency. These factors would certainly influence the base value of a client's ID/debit card.

The information industry would establish a uniform price for each distinct form and type of material in a library's physical collection or available online or otherwise. For instance, children's books and magazines would have a very low price for clients whose type was pre-schooler or youth, and a higher price for educators, adults, and seniors. Higher prices might also be charged pre-schoolers or youth who want to access adult materials. Likewise, materials might have a higher price for employed adults than for unemployed adults, for enterprises than for individuals. One can envision a pricing scheme that is both flexible and fair, based on the type and status of the client, and on the type of library providing the service. This typing of clients and materials is already generally supported by automated circulation systems, and it could be enhanced readily to implement the charging mechanism outlined here.

Each borrower would then be able to use the library and its services up to the value of the debit card in any given year, or other period, without having to pay any additional fees. Any client, however, might add to the value of the card at any time by paying additional sums based on the client's estimate of usage, as well as on usage to date. Any value remaining at the end of a year would be carried over to the next year, so that the client would never lose any funds.

To the extent afforded by data communication networks, clients would be able to use the debit card at any library with appropriate funds transfers between the client's primary library and any other library the client chooses to use. Furthermore, this charging scheme eliminates a great deal of administrative effort and cost that would be incurred for direct cash transactions or for credit card transactions.

Fees collected by the library, or provided from its regular funds, would be apportioned to the author, publisher, distributor, etc., of the materials. In this way, libraries can continue to provide a measure of "free" service to clients according to need and the ability of the library to support such free service, but, at the same time, provide unlimited services to those who have the need and the ability to pay. Present practice prevents many clients from gaining access to data irrespective of their need or ability to pay.

ROLE OF NETWORKS

It will be difficult for libraries to effect these changes so essential for the future, but many libraries already have a mechanism in place through which many of the needed changes can be accomplished, namely regional networks such as AMIGOS, NELINET, and PALINET. The regional networks were established to foster cooperation and resource sharing among their members. Because the networks are, for the most part, membership organizations, each member library is, in effect, part owner of the network. As such, each member is, therefore, entitled to any support and services from the network that the membership believes are required.

Regional networks can assist their members to achieve resource sharing at many levels. For example, networks can, and do, operate shared automation systems in support of two or more member libraries. Networks can implement centralized cataloging on behalf of their members, employ staff whose duties would be to provide shared reference services or shared facilities, and provide specialized staff whose task is to provide service on behalf of member libraries that the members cannot, or should not, provide individually. Networks can, and do, perform cooperative purchasing, contracting, and various administrative and financial services on behalf of their members. Networks can, and do, provide training and continuing education for member staff that is unavailable elsewhere. Regional networks represent a ready-made vehicle for accomplishing much of the previously discussed resource sharing, a vehicle already used to a limited extent by many libraries.

CONCLUSION

Resource sharing, defined broadly, is a way to provide better services to library clients at lower costs. Current and future automation and networking technologies can enhance such resource sharing. These technologies are the means to the service and economic ends libraries must achieve.

The problem of publication pricing and the conflict between data access and the needs of producers for revenues to support their efforts can be addressed effectively through new pricing models for publishers and innovative revenue-generation strategies for libraries. Regional networks do play, and will continue to play, an increasingly important role in assisting libraries to achieve their resource sharing potential.

In a very real sense, this article has outlined the future of information access and delivery in modern cultures. If libraries are to serve as the principal providers of information access and delivery services, innovative and far-sighted management is required to effect true resource sharing and to create the revenue streams necessary to provide information to people when and where they need it.

T - #0198 - 101024 - C0 - 229/152/9 [11] - CB - 9781560243915 - Gloss Lamination